It Happened In Mississippi

It Happened In Series

It Happened In
Mississippi

Remarkable Events That Shaped History

Marlo Carter Kirkpatrick

Guilford, Connecticut

To buy books in quantity for corporate use
or incentives, call **(800) 962-0973**
or e-mail **premiums@GlobePequot.com.**

Map by Alena Joy Pearce © Morris Book Publishing, LLC
Project editor: Lauren Szalkiewicz
Layout: Sue Murray

Library of Congress Cataloging-in-Publication Data is available on file.

ISBN: 978-0-7627-7192-9

Printed in the United States of America

10 9 8 7 6 5 4 3 2 1

CONTENTS

CONTENTS

ACKNOWLEDGMENTS

It Happened in Mississippi could not have been written without the help of many colleagues and friends statewide.

I owe a special thanks to the staff at the Mississippi Department of Archives and History, who is charged with guarding the precious history of our state, and with helping many others like me explore the past that has shaped the Mississippi and Mississippian of today. Thanks also to Cheryl Caldwell May, my research assistant, who spent many hours digging through dusty files and making copies, and as a result, making my job so much easier. I'm also deeply grateful to Tracee Williams, the most patient of editors.

A special thank you goes to Stephen Kirkpatrick. Of all the events that have happened in Mississippi, my favorite was meeting you.

INTRODUCTION

I wasn't born in Mississippi.

Okay, full disclosure—I grew up in Memphis, Tennessee, a city that's a mere eleven-and-a-half miles north of the Mississippi state line. But Mississippi seems to me a million miles away in terms of its unique history, personality, and sheer quirkiness. After more than twenty years with a Mississippi address, the state is as much a part of my soul as of any native daughter's.

Almost anyone who's from around "these parts" or has spent any length of time here will tell you that Mississippi is more than just a spot on the map. It's a state of mind. The remarkable events that have taken place here—events that not only shaped the state, but in many cases, also shaped the nation—will certainly back that up.

Mississippi was the original Wild West, an untamed frontier where adventurous settlers and proud Native Americans battled over the thick woodlands and life-sustaining waterways, and early leaders sometimes made up the rules as they went along. The mythical romance of the Old South was real here as was the dark world of slavery that made it possible. The fate of the nation was determined in Mississippi not once, but twice: first, when the state was rendered a battleground in the 1860s during the Civil War, and again a century later, when brave men and women fought and died during the civil rights movement.

Life has always been a little slower down here. There aren't a lot of distractions, and Mississippi's idea of "hustle and bustle" would likely make a big city dweller laugh out loud. That's probably the reason that Mississippi has always been a hot bed of creativity. Mississippi was the birthplace of the blues, America's only original music, and of Elvis Presley, the King of Rock 'n' Roll. Mississippians have penned some of the world's greatest and most profound literature, resulting in the oft-repeated, tongue-in-cheek mantra, "We might not be able to read, but by gosh, we sure can write." Every four years, the world comes to Mississippi to see the most gifted dancers on earth take the stage during the International Ballet Competition.

Mississippi's landscape itself has also played a notable role in history. The great Mississippi River for which the state was named has been a source of commerce and a source of calamity, and the same Gulf of Mexico that gave the state its sun-spangled waters and white sand beaches spawned the deadly nightmare that was Hurricane Katrina. Other strange phenomena in the state, from catastrophic fires to the music of a rushing river, have been blamed on witchcraft and supernatural happenings.

Revered Mississippi son William Faulkner wrote, "The past isn't dead. It isn't even past." Mississippi's history is present everywhere—in her land, her people, and her culture. But that doesn't mean that Mississippi is stuck in the bygone days. Instead, it's a reminder that all that has transpired here—every game-changing event, every new idea unveiled, and every life lesson learned, including the harsh ones, have influenced Mississippi's present and will continue to shape Mississippi's future.

As you peruse the pages of *It Happened in Mississippi,* I hope you find yourself caught up in the state's storied past, yet longing to hear of new, even more remarkable tales yet to unfold here in the years to come.

HERNANDO DE SOTO CROSSES THE MISSISSIPPI RIVER

1540

While he came to the New World in search of gold, Spanish explorer Hernando de Soto (1496–1542) is best known for his discovery of the Mississippi River. An experienced Spanish conquistador who had played a starring role in the exploration of Central America and the vanquishing of the Inca Empire in Peru, de Soto was commissioned by King Charles I of Spain to lead the first European expedition deep into the region of the southeastern United States then known as "Florida."

By the mid-1530s, de Soto's exploits in Panama, Nicaragua, Honduras, and particularly Peru had made him a wealthy man. De Soto took his portion of the gold plundered from the Inca and returned to Seville, Spain, where he established a luxurious home, complete with a staff of ushers, pages, and other servants. In 1537 he married Isabel de Bobadilla, the daughter of his former patron and a relative of a confidante of Queen Isabella.

While he had planned to enjoy a comfortable life in Spain, rumors of the vast riches waiting in the area then called Florida reawakened both de Soto's ambition and his sense of adventure. De Soto sold his property and invested the proceeds in equipping what was to be a four-year expedition to the New World. King Charles granted de Soto the title of Governor of Cuba and agreed that in addition to a portion of the gold, silver, and other riches de Soto might acquire, he would also receive a sizable piece of land and the title of marquis of the territory he would conquer there on behalf of Spain.

In May of 1539 de Soto sailed from Spain to Cuba, then on to Florida with the best-equipped expedition that had ever attempted a conquest in the New World. The nine-ship expedition included more than six hundred well-armed soldiers, as well as a contingent of priests, craftsmen, and physicians. Also on board were hundreds of horses and war dogs, pigs that would serve as food, and enough supplies to last for several months. The expedition dropped anchor in modern-day Tampa Bay. From there de Soto and his men began their exploration of the wild, unknown frontier to the north and west.

While de Soto's exploits in Central America and Peru had earned him a reputation as a courageous leader and fearless fighter, his dealings with the native people had also made him notorious for his brutality. Spanish expeditions of the era often proclaimed their intention to convert the Native American "heathens" to the Catholic faith, but de Soto instead told the native people that he was a "sun god," an immortal who could not be killed and must be obeyed. As they made their way from Florida through present-day Georgia and Alabama, de Soto and his men took hundreds of Native Americans captive as slaves and killed thousands more, often without justification.

When a hard year's exploration yielded no gold, de Soto sent a contingent of his men with orders to return by ship to Havana for additional supplies, and then meet him in the area of present-day

Pensacola Bay. De Soto and the remaining land party continued south. In an area of what is now Alabama, de Soto met and initially befriended Chief Tuscaluza, possibly with an eye toward kidnapping the chieftain and holding him for ransom, a hallmark of previous de Soto expeditions in Central America and Peru. The plan failed; Chief Tuscaluza summoned thousands of Indian warriors to attack the Spanish expedition near present-day Mobile. The ensuing battle lasted for some nine hours. While the Spanish ultimately prevailed, their victory came at a high price. At least seventy of the Spaniards were killed and nearly all of the surviving officers and men, including de Soto himself, were wounded.

Injured from the battle, exhausted by the hardships and long marches they had endured, and disappointed by their failure to find gold, several of de Soto's men plotted to commandeer the supply ships that waited on the Gulf Coast and sail to Mexico. When he learned of their plot, de Soto changed his plans, leading the men northwest and into the interior, assuring them all the while that they would discover gold.

In December of 1540 de Soto and his remaining men crossed into what is now Mississippi, camping for the winter in an area of present-day Lee County. In the early spring the Native Americans once again mounted an attack, killing more of the men and destroy-ing most of their weapons and supplies. The surviving Spaniards continued northwest, driven now not by the futile search for gold, but by the search for food.

By May of 1541 the once great expedition had been reduced to a small, starving, bedraggled band of men desperate to return to civilization. Yet de Soto continued to urge them on. In late May they reached the banks of the mighty Mississippi River in present-day Tunica County. De Soto, however, was not impressed by the sight of the New World's largest river. Instead, he saw "El Rio de la Florida," the name he gave the Mississippi River, as just the latest in the long list of impediments to the expedition's progress.

While de Soto is typically credited with "discovering" the Mississippi River, many historians argue that he was not the first European to lay eyes upon the mighty river for which the ground where he stood would later be named. Some believe that explorer Alonso Alvarez de Pineda had first seen the great river in 1519. De Soto and his men, however, were inarguably the first Europeans to cross the Mississippi River, building rafts and small boats and floating into present-day Arkansas.

For several months the men explored areas west of the river, but once again failing to discover gold and in growing fear of the hostile Native Americans, de Soto's men demanded that they return south toward the ships they hoped would take them home. Defeated and exhausted, de Soto acquiesced. But in May or June of 1542, before he could cross back over the Mississippi River, de Soto succumbed to a fatal fever. Realizing he was dying, de Soto named a successor to lead the expedition. Five days later, the great conquistador died.

According to some accounts, his men initially buried de Soto, but recalling that he had told the Native Americans he was an immortal "sun god," they realized that if his body was discovered, the Native Americans would launch another attack. They disinterred their leader's body, weighted it with sand and rocks, and sank it in the Mississippi River.

The surviving Spaniards, now more eager than ever to leave the area, tried and failed to reach Mexico over land. They eventually returned to the Mississippi River and built boats that they used to float downstream. Those who survived reached the Mexican coast late in 1543.

From the point of view of the Spanish, de Soto's expedition was a colossal failure. They found no gold, they founded no colonies, and the majority of the men died. But history has been much kinder to de Soto. Over the centuries, reports of his brutality toward the Native Americans have been downplayed in favor of the legend of the brave explorer who discovered the Mississippi River and was buried in its depths.

In 1836 Congress commissioned a dramatic canvas titled *Discovery of the Mississippi* by artist William Henry Powell, which today hangs in the rotunda of the US Capitol building. The last of eight large historical paintings in the rotunda, the work depicts de Soto, riding a white horse and dressed in Renaissance finery, arriving at the Mississippi River as a Native American chief offers a peace pipe.

The city of Hernando and DeSoto County were named in memory of the famous explorer who became Mississippi's first European "tourist." The story of de Soto's adventure in the state is told in sweeping oil murals hanging inside the DeSoto County courthouse. Painted by muralist Newton Alonzo Wells in 1902, the oil paintings originally hung in a hotel in nearby Memphis, Tennessee. Donated to DeSoto County and installed in the courthouse in 1953, the oil paintings carry an estimated value of $700,000—an appropriate tribute to the famed conquistador and to the promise of wealth and riches that drew Hernando de Soto to the New World.

THE LEGEND OF THE SINGING RIVER

1763

South Mississippi's Pascagoula watershed is the largest unimpeded river system in the continental United States, a self-contained, complex ecosystem untouched by damming or similar human efforts to control it. The river takes its name from the Pascagoula Indians, one of many smaller Native American tribes that once populated Mississippi along with larger tribes like the Natchez, Choctaw, Chickasaw, and Biloxi. But according to legend, the Pascagoula Indians gave the river more than just its name. They also gave these waters the ability to sing.

The first record of the Pascagoula Indians is found in the 1699 writings of Pierre Le Moyne d'Iberville, a French explorer who established a colony at what is now Biloxi. Upon landing on the Mississippi Gulf Coast in February of 1699, d'Iberville met Indians of the "Biloccy" (Biloxi), which meant "first people" and Pascagoula, which meant "bread people" tribes, who lived in villages along the shores of the Pascagoula River and along the Mississippi Gulf Coast.

Even in d'Iberville's day, the Pascagoula were a small tribe, believed to consist of no more than a hundred families. After the British took the Mississippi area from the French in 1763, the Pascagoula disappeared from the Gulf Coast area. Historians and anthropologists believe they moved west across the Mississippi River into Louisiana or were absorbed by the larger Chickasaw or Choctaw tribes, but legend tells another story of the demise of the Pascagoula.

According to Indian oral traditions, a Biloxi Indian princess named Anola was betrothed to a hot-tempered Biloxi warrior, but she fell in love instead with Altama, a chieftain of the Pascagoula tribe. When the gentle Pascagoula people offered the young lovers sanctuary, the spurned Biloxi warrior mounted an attack on the Pascagoula. Rather than face death or slavery at the hands of the Biloxi, the entire Pascagoula tribe joined hands and walked into the Pascagoula River, singing the traditional tribal death chant as they surrendered their souls to the waters. Over the centuries since, the Pascagoula River has joined them in their mournful song.

How much of the legend is true remains forever a mystery, but whether the source is Indian ghosts or scientific phenomena, the Pascagoula River *does* sing. Its "music" has been compared to everything from the buzzing of bees to the strains of a harp. The song reaches its highest volume on late summer and early autumn evenings; at times the river's song has been loud enough to stop traffic on the Pascagoula River bridge.

Whether it's a trick of the sand and silt or the haunting chant of a tribe long extinct, a concert performed by the Pascagoula River is an experience available only in Mississippi.

THE ARREST AND ARRAIGNMENT
OF AARON BURR

1807

From his rise to power as the third vice president of the United States to his trial for treason, Aaron Burr was one of the most controversial of the early American political figures.

Born in 1756 in Newark, New Jersey, Burr was admitted to the College of New Jersey, now known as Princeton, at the age of thirteen. Burr served as an officer in the American Revolution, achieving status as a war hero for his daring exploits on the battlefield. Following his military service, Burr completed law school and launched an illustrious political career. He was elected to the New York State Assembly, appointed New York State Attorney General, voted a US Senator; he reached the pinnacle of his political career in 1801, when he was elected vice president of the United States under President Thomas Jefferson.

Burr's career began a downward spiral in 1804, the last year of his vice presidency, when he challenged his political rival, US founding father Alexander Hamilton, to a duel. Burr and Hamilton had once been friends, but political differences had driven a wedge between them. Their relationship continued to deteriorate over nearly a decade, with Hamilton quoted by a second party in a New York newspaper as saying that Burr was "a dangerous man, and one who ought not be trusted with the reins of government." Burr responded by challenging Hamilton to a duel in New Jersey during which Hamilton was killed.

While Burr was never tried for the illegal duel, Hamilton's controversial death ended Burr's political career. When President Jefferson dropped him from the 1804 ticket, Burr left Washington, traveling west, where he believed he could make a fresh start after this fall from political grace. He wrote to his son-in-law, "I am to be disfranchised, and in New Jersey, hanged. Having substantial objection to both, I shall not at present hazard either, but shall seek another country."

In that era, "west" included the newly acquired Territory of Louisiana, whose borders were still disputed by Spain. Adventurous, ambitious Americans in that region were eager to expand western settlement into adjacent territories still occupied by Spain, causing friction that threatened to lead to a war between Spain and the United States. The unstable political climate lent itself to intrigue and offered opportunities for men willing to take risks.

Burr began explorations in the west, leasing large tracts of land from Spain, raising funds, and recruiting financial backers and volunteers for a campaign in the area. His primary contacts included Harman Blennerhassett, a wealthy landowner who provided funds and a staging point for men and supplies on his island estate in the Ohio River, and General James Wilkinson, the governor of the Louisiana Territory. Burr also met with Anthony Merry, Britain's minister to the United States, offering to help "effect a separation of the western part of the United States" from the rest of the country if a partnership could be arranged.

Reports of Burr's activities in the west began appearing in newspaper articles, which suggested that he was raising and equipping an army in preparation for some type of military endeavor. Later, Burr would claim he was only preparing himself and a group of fellow western settlers in the event the United States went to war with Spain, but rumors began circulating that Burr was planning to establish a separate confederacy of western states and territories with himself as its leader. By early 1806 President Thomas Jefferson had begun receiving messages from multiple sources telling him that his former vice president was planning the overthrow of his administration.

Historians remain divided as to what Burr's ultimate intentions might have been, but his plans collapsed before they truly began. Burr and Wilkinson had begun corresponding in "cipher," a secret code that used numbers in place of letters. Believing Burr's plans of a western conquest would fail and seeing possible charges against himself ahead, Wilkinson turned informer. He sent President Jefferson what he claimed was a translation of a letter in cipher from Burr outlining plans to mount an attack in the Spanish territories. Wilkinson also told Jefferson that Burr was raising an army to begin a revolution against the United States in the west, with the ultimate plan of severing the western territories and establishing a new government in the former Spanish and US western territories with Burr as its head.

President Jefferson ordered Burr arrested and tried for the capital crime of treason. Burr's "army" disintegrated as Wilkinson began rounding up suspects and potential witnesses for the pending trial. Meanwhile, Burr was sailing down the Mississippi River with a hundred of his men, where he expected to find ships and supplies ordered by Wilkinson waiting for him at New Orleans. Only upon reaching Bayou Pierre, thirty miles above Natchez, did Burr learn that Wilkinson had turned from his coconspirator into his pursuer. A friend handed Burr a New Orleans newspaper that featured a translation of the coded letter Burr had sent to Wilkinson and advertised a reward for the capture of "Aaron Burr, wanted for treason."

Burr responded by sending a letter to Cowles Mead, the acting governor of the Mississippi Territory, avowing his innocence and according to Mead, "solicited me to appease the fears which his approach had begotten; at the same time, he . . . induced me to adopt a different mode of conduct." Mead, however, was taking no chances. In a letter to President Jefferson, Mead wrote that, "Instead of adopting [Burr's] pacific admonition, I ordered a very large portion of the militia of the territory to rendezvous . . . and in 24 hours, I had the honor to review 375 men at Natchez, prepared to defend their country."

Days later, Mead himself went to meet with Burr at his camp. "After a lengthy interview," Mead wrote to President Jefferson, "he offered to surrender himself to the civil authority of the territory, and to suffer his boats to be searched. . . . Col. Burr, accompanied by my aids, Majors Shields and Poindexter, rode down to the place, and was committed to the highest tribunal of the civil authority, where he now remains for trial."

Mead seemed disappointed, however, in the lack of evidence against Burr found upon his surrender. "Thus, sir," he wrote to President Jefferson, "this mighty alarm, with all its exaggerations, has eventuated in nine boats, and one hundred men, and the major part of these are boys, or young men just from school. Many of their depositions have been taken before Judge Rodney, but they bespeak ignorance of the views or designs of the colonel. I believe them really ignorant and deluded. I believe they are the dupes of stratagem, if the asseverations of General Wilkinson are to be accredited."

Following his surrender, Burr was escorted to the nearby town of Washington, the capital of the Mississippi Territory, where he would be arraigned by the Supreme Court of the Territory on charges of treason. While awaiting the court proceedings, Burr was held in custody, or by some accounts, was a "guest," at Windy Hill Manor, the home of Colonel Benaijah Osmun, a wealthy planter and friend of Burr's who was convinced of his innocence. Osmun was not alone; according to reports from the day, "[Burr's] arrest occasioned great agitation in the Territory, many regarding him as a victim of the President's jealousy. Some even eulogized him, demanding his prompt discharge, hoping to share in what they believed to be his schemes."

In February of 1807 the court convened at Jefferson College, the first educational institution chartered in the Mississippi Territory and an institution named after Burr's antagonist, Thomas Jefferson. After hearing the evidence against Burr, the grand jury declared Burr "not guilty of any crime or misdemeanor against the United States."

Burr demanded and received his release. But when additional information about Burr's activities came to light, a new warrant was issued. Burr was once again arrested and this time was transported to Richmond, Virginia, where he was charged with treason for assembling an armed force to take New Orleans and separate the western territories from the Atlantic states. He was also charged with a misdemeanor for sending a military expedition against territories belonging to Spain, a country at peace with the United States. The subsequent, dramatic trial ended in acquittal, when Justice John Marshall ruled that Burr's actions, although improper, did not fit the strict definition of "treason" outlined in the US Constitution.

But while Burr won in the courtroom, he lost in the court of public opinion. His schemes in the west left him with large debts, few friends, and in a state of disgrace. In a final quest he left the United States for Europe, where he tried unsuccessfully to convince Britain and France to support other efforts to take land in North America. Burr remained overseas until 1812, when he returned to the United States to practice law in New York City under his mother's family name of "Edwards." There he spent the remainder of his life in relative obscurity.

Today, Historic Jefferson College, the site of Burr's arraignment, is a museum. Its redbrick buildings and Georgian-style architecture tucked into the wilderness, Jefferson College still looks much as it did when the militia delivered Burr for his trial more than two hundred years ago. Two great oak trees known as the "Aaron Burr Oaks" grace the entrance to Jefferson College. Over the centuries the legend has grown that the trees were so named because Burr was tried in their shadow. In reality, according to docents at Historic Jefferson College, the trees were not planted until 1839, thirty-two years after the trial. But the Aaron Burr Oaks they remain, a reminder of the price one man paid for allegedly attempting to overthrow the US government.

WILLIAM JOHNSON
IS FREED

1820

William Johnson was a successful, popular businessman and slave owner in Natchez in the early 1800s. While that description fit many men in the wealthy river town, Johnson's biography offered a unique twist that set him apart from other business leaders of the day—Johnson, a former slave himself, was black.

William Johnson was not the only free black man living in Natchez during the antebellum years in the South. Between 1820 and 1860 the Natchez area was home to the majority of Mississippi's free black population, which by 1840 included approximately 1,400 men and women who had purchased their own emancipation or been freed by their owners.

What made Johnson stand out in a group of people already living in an unusual circumstance were his writings. Johnson kept a diary chronicling his daily life in Natchez. Found in the attic of his former home in 1938, Johnson's diary provided a rare, firsthand glimpse into the lives of free blacks in the antebellum South. In 1951 the diary was released in the form of a book titled *William Johnson's Natchez: The Diary of a Free Negro.*

Johnson was born a slave in 1809. In 1820 eleven-year-old William, his mother, Amy, and sister, Adelia, were granted their freedom by their owner, a white man also named William Johnson whom most historians believe was the younger Johnson's father. Ten years later, after serving as an apprentice under his brother-in-law, James Miller, Johnson bought Miller's barbershop in Natchez for three hundred dollars. He began a thriving business, part of which included teaching the art of barbering to other young, free, black men, and soon earned the nickname, "the barber of Natchez."

Around this same time, Johnson began keeping a diary, a practice he would continue until his death in 1851. The diary chronicles Johnson's growing commercial and personal successes in Natchez. Energetic and business savvy, he soon became a prosperous businessman. By 1835 Johnson's initial investment of three hundred dollars had grown to three thousand. That same year he married Ann Battles, a free black woman. Over the years he diversified his business, opening multiple barbershops, all staffed by black barbers and all servicing white customers—as many as fifty per day. He began speculating in farmland and commercial rental properties, opened a bathhouse, and even loaned small amounts of money to white businessmen, charging them interest on the loans.

Despite his personal history, Johnson felt no compunction to keeping slaves, at one point owning at least sixteen black men and women. He even hired out his slaves as manual labor, launching a coal and sand hauling company in Natchez. Johnson's diary held several entries about his slaves, including multiple, exasperated descriptions of a slave named Stephen, who had a penchant for getting intoxicated and running away. Johnson recounted, "I went to the stable and gave him a pretty sefveere [sic] thrashing with the cowhide—then he was perfectly calm and quite [sic] and could then do his work. Tis singular how much good it does some people to get whipped [sic]." Another entry noted that, "I today saw a man up at the auction room and he wanted to buy my girl Sarah. I told him he could have her for twelve hundred dollars in cash."

A remarkable entry described Johnson's visit to the Forks of the Road, one of the antebellum South's busiest slave markets. Located at an intersection near downtown Natchez, Forks of the Road sometimes displayed as many as five hundred slaves for sale. Johnson's diary entry for May 14, 1841, noted, "I rode out this afternoon to the Forks of the Road to try and swop [sic] Stephen off for someone else, but could find no one that I like." The offhand way in which Johnson described his visit to the market clearly indicated his comfort and security in his position in Natchez. Like the other businesspeople, he was there to browse and had no fear of being mistaken for a slave himself. A few years later, Johnson sold Stephen, but wrote that as he closed the transaction, "many tears was in my eyes today on account of my selling poor Steven [sic]. I felt hurt, but liquor is the cause of his troubles. I would not have parted with him if he had only let liquor alone, but he cannot do it."

Johnson's diary entries also referenced his family, which grew to include ten children. Johnson and his wife sent several of their children to New Orleans to study in a school for free blacks, baptizing and registering them with a local church to guard against the potential they might be kidnapped and sold into slavery. While Johnson was devoted to his wife and family, one entry did make mention of "several quarrels with my wife. She commenced it, of course."

Johnson penned colorful passages about Natchez gossip, duels and quarrels, and his many pastimes. He enjoyed hunting, fishing, target shooting, shopping at auctions, gambling on horse races, and playing marbles. He sought to further his knowledge, subscribing to many magazines and newspapers, and invested the money he earned in elegant clothing and furnishings. Johnson became a prominent, active citizen, and enjoyed the respect of his neighbors both black and white.

Johnson's May 7, 1840, entry read, "Today was in the aforenoon very pleasant day until past one o'clock and then we had rain, with one of the greatest tornadoes that ever was seen in this place before . . ." The tornado tore through downtown Natchez, killing three hundred people and destroying large swaths of the city. Johnson's entry for May 8 noted, "Several persons found during this day that was killed under the houses. Oh, what times, no one ever seen such times." Johnson used brick, windows, and doors salvaged from the wreckage to construct a new home on Natchez's State Street, finishing the interior walls with plaster reinforced from human hair gathered in his barbershops. The building would serve as home for his descendants for over a century.

In 1851 a boundary dispute between Johnson and another free black man, Baylor Winn, landed the two men in court. When the judge ruled in Johnson's favor, Winn was furious. Winn later ambushed Johnson and shot him. Johnson died the following day.

An article in the Natchez *Concordian Intelligencier* described the "dreadful murder" of "Mr. William Johnson, an esteemed citizen, and long known as the proprietor of the fashionable barber's shop on Main Street. . . . The funeral of Mr. Johnson was attended by a numerous procession on Wednesday morning, the Rev. Mr. Watkins of the Methodist Church performing the religious services. This event has made a deep and painful impression upon our community."

The *Natchez Courier* noted:

> *What could only be deemed a horrible and deliberate murder had been committed upon an excellent and most inoffensive man. It was ascertained that William Johnson, a free man of color born and raised in Natchez, and holding a respected position on account of his character, intelligence and deportment, had been shot. . . . His funeral services . . . paid a just tribute to his memory, holding up his example as one well worthy of imitation by all of his class.*

There was no question as to who had pulled the trigger; not only had Johnson lived long enough to name Winn as the guilty party, but there were witnesses to the murder. Winn, however, argued that his part-Indian ancestry meant that he was actually more white than black. Therefore, according to Mississippi law of the day, the young black boys who had witnessed the murder were prohibited by law from testifying against Winn. The case then hinged on whether Winn was indeed white or black. When two hung juries could not come to an agreement on Winn's race, he was allowed to walk free.

Johnson's three-story, redbrick townhouse on State Street in downtown Natchez was owned by his family until they sold it to the Ellicott Hill Preservation Society in 1976. The house was then donated to the city, and finally to the National Park Service in 1990. In 2005, following an extensive restoration process, the National Park Service opened the house as a museum and tribute to the life of William Johnson, the barber of Natchez.

THE TREATY OF
DANCING RABBIT CREEK

1830

The land surrounding present-day Choctaw is sacred to the Choctaw Indians for good reason. According to Indian legend, the entire Choctaw nation was born at the Nanih Waiya Historic Site, an ancient area marked by ceremonial Indian mounds just off Mississippi Highway 21. The Choctaw refer to a large mound on the site as the "Mother Mound," and a sacred cave nearby is said to be the very spot where the first Choctaw Indian entered the world.

The tribe can trace its history in Mississippi back as far as the time of Christ. For centuries afterward, the Choctaws enjoyed their status as the largest Native American tribe in Mississippi, with as many as thirty thousand Choctaws inhabiting fifty villages in the center of the state. But by the early 1800s, the Choctaws' reign in Mississippi had come to an end, with white settlers far outnumbering the dwindling population of Native Americans. A series of treaties over the years had gradually but steadily reduced the amount of land the Choctaws could still claim as their own.

In the late 1820s following President Andrew Jackson's federal policy of Indian removal from United States' lands, Mississippi Governor Gerard Brandon and the state legislature called for the extension of state law into Choctaw and Chickasaw lands and the final expulsion of the Indian nations from Mississippi. The policy of removing all Indians east of the Mississippi River was firmly in place. The Choctaws were faced with the choice of forgoing their independence and tribal customs by submitting to the white man's law or of moving to lands west of the Mississippi River where they could preserve their tribal government and customs.

At this time the Choctaws were led by three chiefs, section chiefs Mashulatubbee and Nittahachi and section chief Greenwood LeFlore, who had also been elected chief of the entire Choctaw nation. The son of a French Canadian trader and businessman and a woman of Choctaw and French descent, LeFlore had received a fine education in Nashville through the auspices of a family friend. He was elected chief of the Choctaws at the age of twenty-two and soon proved himself a capable and progressive leader. The other chiefs were older and clung more to the traditional Choctaw beliefs. Under the sometimes-divided leadership of the three, the Choctaws agreed to meet with President Jackson's representatives, Secretary of War John Eaton and John Coffee, to negotiate a treaty.

Jackson's representatives and the Choctaw leaders met in September of 1830 at Dancing Rabbit Creek in present-day Noxubee County. The meeting included an audience of approximately six thousand Choctaws, who clearly understood the importance of the meeting to the future of their people as a nation. The federal government provided food for all in attendance over the course of the multiday meeting. There was also an abundance of whiskey, as well as "gaming tables and every cunning contrivance" that might lessen the Choctaws' resolve to keep their land. In fact the only people forbidden to attend the meeting where the missionaries who had come with their Choctaw Christian converts, but who were asked to leave by the government officials because "their religious instruction would have a tendency to distract the Indians' minds."

The three Choctaw leaders were a study in wardrobe contrasts. Thirty-year-old LeFlore wore a standard business suit. Nittahachi came in full traditional garb, complete with intricate Choctaw beadwork, while Mashulatubbee, who apparently had a fascination with uniforms, wore a blue uniform sent to him as a gift from President Jackson.

Coffee and Eaton had been sent with clear instructions from President Jackson to come back with a treaty. No excuses would be accepted, and no limitations had been placed on their methods of acquiring it. Eaton opened his remarks by saying, "It is not your lands, but your happiness that we seek to obtain." When flattery failed, he changed tactics, warning, "The Choctaws had no choice . . . but were bound to sell their land and remove. If they refused, the president in 20 days would march with an army . . . build forts in their hunting grounds . . . Their lands would be seized." As negotiations wore on, Eaton's words grew more dire. He concluded by saying that if they did not reach an agreement, the Choctaws "would become paupers and beggars, broken up and utterly destroyed as a nation."

LeFlore was a realist who understood that the Choctaws would be removed; it was only a matter of how soon and under what circumstances. If the Choctaws accepted the treaty, LeFlore realized, conditions would likely be more favorable than if they rejected it. LeFlore negotiated to have several articles added to the treaty, including Article XIV, which made provisions for those Choctaws who wished to remain in their homeland under Mississippi law. Under that article each remaining family would be given 640 acres of land. With Article XIV included, LeFlore agreed to sign. Frightened by Eaton's dire threats, the other district chiefs also made their marks.

Article I of the final Treaty of Dancing Rabbit Creek read, "Perpetual peace and friendship is pledged and agreed upon, by and between the United States, and the Mingoes, Chiefs and Warriors of the Choctaw Nation of Red People." The treaty went on to provide that the Choctaws would surrender all of their remaining lands in Mississippi in exchange for an area west of the Mississippi River. They would be given three years in which to relocate. The treaty specified, "In wagons, and with steamboats, as may be found necessary, the United States agree to remove the Indians to their new homes, at their expense, and under the care of discreet and careful persons, who will be kind and brotherly to them."

As a result of the Treaty of Dancing Rabbit Creek, the central area of Mississippi, about one-third of the state's entire land, was opened for white settlement. The treaty also spelled the end of the independent Choctaw Nation in Mississippi. In 1832 the Choctaws were moved from Mississippi to the unorganized "Indian Territory" west of the river in present-day Oklahoma. Unfortunately, the treaty was poorly executed. Government officials had no concept of how to organize a massive exodus of thousands of Indians into a new land, or how to provide for them until they could once again take care of themselves. While the white Americans who helped with the relocation were supposed to be "kind and brotherly to them," the move was traumatic for the Choctaws. The forced movement, along with the subsequent removal of the Cherokee nation in 1838, came to be known as "the Trail of Tears."

Those Choctaws who remained in Mississippi also suffered as a result of the treaty. According to Article XIV, the Indians had six months in which to register for the land to which they were entitled. The Indian agent appointed to supervise the registration process was a known drunkard who frequently forgot to open the registration office, failed to properly register the Indians, and loaned out the registration books, resulting in the theft of land by white men who simply scratched out the rightful Choctaw owners' names. Greenwood LeFlore twice traveled to Washington and met personally with President Andrew Jackson, requesting that Jackson right the wrongs inflicted upon his people. But with his treaty in hand, the president did little to intervene.

The remaining Choctaws were eventually relocated to the Choctaw Indian Reservation near Philadelphia where their descendents live today. The modern Choctaws have built a thriving community anchored by the Pearl River Resort, a large casino and entertainment complex.

Unlike former Choctaw chief Mushulatubbee and other tribal leaders who chose to migrate along the Trail of Tears rather than submit to Mississippi law, Chief Greenwood LeFlore remained in Mississippi. His leadership role in negotiating the treaty was rewarded with 2,500 acres of farmland in the Mississippi Delta, which eventually became LeFlore County. Here Greenwood LeFlore became a prosperous planter, running a large operation supported by slave labor and residing in a mansion he named "Malmaison." Many of the Choctaws turned against LeFlore, blaming him for their misfortune and resenting his financial success and comfortable lifestyle, which stood in stark contrast not only to their own, but also to that of many white men. Despite his critics, LeFlore remained a popular figure among the white population. He was elected to the Mississippi Legislature and eventually built a small business community he christened "Point LeFlore."

But LeFlore never turned from his Choctaw roots. Until his later years, his friends and family referred to him as "Old Chief." When he died in 1865, Greenwood LeFlore was buried wrapped in an American flag beneath a tomb bearing the inscription, "Greenwood LeFlore, the last chief of the Choctaws east of the Mississippi."

THE GIBRALTAR OF THE CONFEDERACY

1863

From 1862 to 1863, Mississippi was a bloody battleground, a focal point of conflict during the American Civil War. Fifteen key battles and dozens of skirmishes were waged on Mississippi soil. Men were killed, property was destroyed, and a once prosperous state was reduced to ruin, a conquered land occupied by enemy forces that had once been countrymen. Key battles were waged at Corinth, Brice's Cross Roads, Tupelo, Raymond, and Champion Hill, but the most notable Civil War conflict took place at Vicksburg.

President Abraham Lincoln called this city high on the bluffs of the Mississippi River "the key . . . let us get Vicksburg and all that country is ours. The war can never be brought to a close until that key is in our pocket." A victory at Vicksburg would sever Texas, Arkansas, and Louisiana from the Confederacy and give the Union complete control of the Mississippi River.

Led by General Ulysses S. Grant, the Union army's campaign to capture Vicksburg lasted from the spring of 1862 until the summer of 1863. For over a year, Vicksburg seemed impregnable as Union forces made several fruitless attempts by land and water to capture the heavily fortified city. Its refusal to fall earned Vicksburg the nickname, "the Gibraltar of the Confederacy."

On May 1, 1863, Grant won a key battle at Port Gibson, Mississippi, and moved quickly inland, marching northeast toward Edwards and the Southern Railroad of Mississippi, the vital supply line that connected Vicksburg with the city of Jackson and points east. Meanwhile, Union forces won a battle at Raymond, captured Jackson, and defeated General John C. Pemberton's main army at Champion Hill and the Big Black River.

Pemberton retreated into Vicksburg and Grant followed. The Union army surrounded the city from north to east to south, while the Union navy floated on the river below. As Pemberton's army of 30,000 retreated into Vicksburg, many women, children, and other noncombatants tried to flee the city, but with all roads out of town leading straight into Grant's army, there was nowhere to run.

Diarist Emma Balfour, a doctor's wife whose home in the city provided a front row seat to the Confederate retreat, wrote, "I hope never to witness again such a scene. From twelve o'clock until late in the night, the streets and roads were jammed with wagons, cannons, horses, men, mules, stock, sheep, everything you can imagine that appertains to an army being brought hurriedly within the entrenchment. . . . What is to become of all the living things in this place when the boats commence shelling, God only knows. [We are] shut up as in a trap—no ingress or egress—and thousands of women and children."

When direct charges against the city failed, Grant decided to starve Vicksburg into submission. Union troops surrounded the city by land and by river and for the next forty-seven days and nights engaged in "the grand sport of tossing giant shells into Vicksburg."

Perched high atop a hill, the Vicksburg courthouse was a favorite target for shelling until all of the Union prisoners held in Vicksburg were moved into the courtroom—a ploy credited with saving the building. A similar tactic was employed at Duff Green, a mansion that had been converted into a field hospital. When the shelling began, the injured Confederates were moved to the basement while the Union wounded were relocated to the roof. To this day antebellum homes in Vicksburg, many now operating as bed-and-breakfast inns, still bear battle scars in the form of cannon balls embedded in the walls.

As the bombardment continued, the frightened citizens of Vicksburg took shelter in caves dug into nearby hillsides. Some caves were simple, one-room shelters, while others were multiroom suites that included parlors and bedrooms outfitted with furniture and carpets from the owners' fine homes.

Balfour wrote, "Just as we got in, several . . . [shells] exploded . . . just over our heads. As all this rushed over me and the sense of suffocation from being underground, the certainty that there was no way of escape, that we were hemmed in, caged, for one moment my heart seemed to stand still. Nearly all the families in town spent the night in their caves."

Vicksburg resident Mary Loughborough also penned vivid scenes of her experience in the caves. "I ran to the entrance to call the servants in, and immediately after they entered, a shell struck the earth a few feet from the entrance, burying itself without exploding. I ran to the little dressing room, and could hear them striking around us on all sides. One fell near the cave entrance, and a servant boy grabbed it and threw it outside; it never exploded. And so the weary days went on . . . when we could not tell in what terrible form death might come to us before the sun went down."

And yet, Vicksburg refused to surrender. Balfour wrote, "The general impression is that they fire at this city, in that way thinking that they will wear out the women and children and sick, and General Pemberton will be impatient to surrender the place on that account. But they little know the spirit of the Vicksburg women and children if they expect this."

Soldiers and citizens suffered alike as the siege wore on. The summer heat was terrible, food and water supplies dwindled, and mule meat became a delicacy. As the long, sweltering days passed, the distance between the enemy lines shrank, until Union aggressors and Confederate defenders were camped virtually eyeball-to-eyeball. During lulls in the shelling, soldiers from opposite sides exchanged jokes and stories along with coffee and tobacco, and two brothers from Missouri fighting on opposite sides were temporarily reunited.

Then on July 3, 1863, with his army and the civilian population starving and no hope of reinforcements from outside the city, General Pemberton met with General Grant to discuss terms of surrender. When Grant demanded his usual unconditional surrender, Pemberton replied, "Sir, it is unnecessary that you and I hold any further conversation. We will go to fighting again at once. I can assure you, you will bury many more of your men before you will enter Vicksburg." Weary of the siege and eager to claim victory, Grant relented, offering parole to the city's defenders.

On July 4, 1863, the Confederate flag flying high over the river was lowered, and the Stars and Stripes once again flew over Vicksburg. More than one hundred years would pass before the city of Vicksburg would again celebrate the Fourth of July.

Even though starving and exhausted, the Confederates defending the city were outraged by the surrender. Many of the Rebel soldiers destroyed their arms, scattering the ammunition on the ground rather than surrendering it to the Union troops, and tore their battle standards into shreds. In a remarkable show of respect for the defenders, the Union troops refrained from taunting the vanquished. Instead, according to one witness, the Federal troops entered the war-torn city with a "hearty cheer for the gallant defenders of Vicksburg," and food and water were offered with the sentiment, "Here, brave Reb, I know you are starved nearly to death."

For the remainder of the war, Vicksburg was an occupied city and a regional base for Union operations. Despite the ferocity of the Union attack and the more than 22,000 shells fired into the city, the town reported less than a dozen civilian casualties. But combined with the Confederate defeat at Gettysburg, the surrender of Vicksburg spelled the end of the Confederacy. With the fall of Vicksburg, the Union forces gained control of the Mississippi River from Cairo, Illinois, to the Gulf of Mexico. Upon hearing of the Confederate surrender, President Lincoln wrote, "the Father of Waters again goes unvexed to the sea."

The final days of siege and battle are replayed endlessly today on the green expanses and rolling hills of the Vicksburg National Military Park, where 1,800 acres of fortifications and earthworks lined with great stone monuments tell the dramatic story of the defense and fall of the Gibraltar of the Confederacy. The Confederate and Union lines are identified, and markers trace the progress of the Union soldiers as they pushed uphill under fire in the scorching Mississippi heat. Generals made of stone lead a permanent charge, bronze horses eternally race into battle, and moss-covered cannons guard the bluffs against a final attack.

WHERE FLOWERS
HEALED A NATION

1866

More than one American city may profess to have been the site where
Memorial Day, the federal holiday honoring those killed in military
service, was observed for the first time, but Columbus has a moving
story of loss and healing to back up its claim.

During the American Civil War, many of Columbus's churches
and public buildings were converted to field hospitals. Wounded
from the Battle of Shiloh were treated at Columbus, and hundreds of
Union and Confederate soldiers were laid to rest in the city's sprawl-
ing Odd Fellows Cemetery.

By 1866 the war had ended, but animosity between North and
South still lingered. On April 25 a group of Confederate war widows
helped both sides take a step toward reconciliation. The widows
made a somber trek to Odd Fellows Cemetery laden with wreaths
and garlands with which to decorate the graves of their Confederate
husbands, fathers, brothers, and heroes. Once there, the women were
moved with compassion by the sight of the unadorned graves of the

fallen Union soldiers buried so far from their homes. In a generous gesture of healing, the women decorated the graves of the Union soldiers buried at Odd Fellows as well as those of the Confederates.

A newspaper account of the event read, "We are glad to see that no distinction was made between our own Confederate dead and the Federal soldiers who slept their last sleep by them . . . Confederate and Federals, once enemies, now friends receiving their tribute of respect."

News of the good deed of the ladies of Columbus soon spread nationwide, spurring other communities to follow suit and earning Columbus a reputation as the city "where flowers healed the nation." In recognition of the healing event that had taken place within its gates, Odd Fellows Cemetery was renamed "Friendship."

Francis Miles Finch, a judge in Ithaca, New York, heard of the gesture and wrote a poem to commemorate the occasion. Originally published in *The Atlantic Monthly* in 1867, Finch's "The Blue and the Gray" would be a mainstay of Decoration Day observances for the next decade. The poem read:

> *By the flow of the inland river,*
> *Whence the fleets of iron have fled,*
> *Where the blades of the grave-grass quiver,*
> *Asleep are the ranks of the dead.*

> *Under the sod and the dew,*
> *Waiting the judgment day*
> *Under the one, the Blue,*
> *Under the other, the Gray.*

These in the robings of glory,
Those in the gloom of defeat,
All with the battle-blood gory,
In the dusk of eternity meet.

Under the sod and the dew,
Waiting the judgment day
Under the laurel, the Blue,
Under the willow, the Gray.

From the silence of sorrowful hours
The desolate mourners go,
Lovingly laden with flowers
Alike for the friend and the foe.

Under the sod and the dew,
Waiting the judgment day
Under the roses, the Blue,
Under the lilies, the Gray.

So with an equal splendor,
The morning sun-rays fall,
With a touch impartially tender,
On the blossoms blooming for all.

Under the sod and the dew,
Waiting the judgment day
Broidered with gold, the Blue,
Mellowed with gold, the Gray.

So, when the summer calleth,
On forest and field of grain,
With an equal murmur falleth
The cooling drip of the rain.

Under the sod and the dew,
Waiting the judgment day
Wet with the rain, the Blue
Wet with the rain, the Gray.

Sadly, but not with upbraiding,
The generous deed was done,
In the storm of the years that are fading
No braver battle was won.

Under the sod and the dew,
Waiting the judgment day
Under the blossoms, the Blue,
Under the garlands, the Gray

No more shall the war cry sever,
Or the winding rivers be red;
They banish our anger forever
When they laurel the graves of our dead.

Under the sod and the dew,
Waiting the judgment day
Love and tears for the Blue,
Tears and love for the Gray.

As one of Finch's contemporaries wrote, "all the orations and sermons and appeals for the restoration of kindly feeling between the two sections have been exceeded in real effect upon the national heart by this simple poem."

The Columbus ladies' gesture evolved into a national "Decoration Day," which eventually came to be known as Memorial Day. The first national observance of a Decoration Day came on May 30, 1868, when flowers were placed on the graves of Union and Confederate soldiers at Arlington National Cemetery. In 1967, one hundred years after its original observance in Columbus, federal law officially named the event "Memorial Day."

Today, Friendship Cemetery is the final resting place of some 16,000 souls, including veterans for the American Revolution, War of 1812, Civil War, Korean War, and Vietnam War, and is listed on the National Register of Historic Places. The gesture that healed a nation is reenacted each April at Friendship Cemetery, when costumed women bearing flowers once again decorate the graves of the Confederate and Union dead, sharing love and tears for the Blue, and tears and love for the Gray.

"YELLOW JACK" INVADES MISSISSIPPI

1878

Yellow fever.

In the 1800s the mere mention of the words was enough to send Mississippians fleeing from their towns and cities, fearful of the dreaded disease that killed thousands in sweeping epidemics throughout the South. Yellow fever victims died a painful, gruesome death, marked by severe headaches and body aches; skyrocketing fever; bleeding from virtually every orifice, including the eyes, ears, nose, and mouth; and violent, projectile retching of copious amounts of black vomit, later understood to be partially digested blood originating from hemorrhaging in the digestive tract. Liver failure led to jaundice and a dramatic yellowing of the victims' skin, giving the feared pestilence its name.

Cases of the "yellow jack," "saffron scourge," "bronze john," or the aptly named "black vomit" were reported in Mississippi as early as 1701, but the worst epidemic in the state's history occurred in 1878, when a yellow fever outbreak of catastrophic proportion swept through the entire Mississippi Valley. The apocalyptic epidemic killed more than 20,000 people, including at least 4,118 Mississippians.

The first case in the historic epidemic was reported in May of 1878 in New Orleans, when a sailor arriving aboard the steamship *Emily B. Souder* fell ill. The news that yellow fever had hit New Orleans prompted one-fifth of the city's population to flee, leaving streets and businesses barren. "Only our mosquitoes keep up the hum of industry," reported the *New Orleans Picayune.* But the epidemic was not contained to Louisiana. The probable source of the disease in Mississippi was the towboat *John Porter,* which docked in Vicksburg with infected crewmen on board. Within days the disease had crippled Vicksburg and begun a relentless, deadly march through the state.

As cases spread throughout the South, tens of thousands of people fled the fever-ravaged cities of New Orleans, Vicksburg, and Memphis, Tennessee, only to find they had nowhere to take refuge. As soon as news of the sickness spread, cities and towns enforced quarantines and yellow fever barricades, posting armed guards to shoot anyone from out-side who might bring the dreaded yellow jack into their cities. Officials at Columbus guarded the banks of the Tombigbee River with orders to "sink any boat hailing from the direction of Mobile, Alabama." With much of the South shut down, the disease traveled with fleeing refugees as far as Kentucky, Indiana, Illinois, and Ohio.

By August of 1878 yellow fever had made its way to Grenada, a city of approximately 2,000 residents in north Mississippi. Nearly half the city's population had already fled in terror; yellow jack infected the majority of those who remained. National attention was focused on Grenada as the disease ravaged the city. A *New York Times* article dated August 15, 1878, painted a grim picture of Grenada as a town in the grip of the "Yellow Angel of Death." Under the headline, "Horrors of Yellow Fever: A Mississippi Town Depopulated," the article described a city in which "all the business houses are closed excepting the drug store and undertakers' shop, and the town presents the appearance of a deserted graveyard. No trains on either road are allowed to stop here, and the town is completely quarantined."

Reports from Grenada cited the high number of dying left uncared for and the higher number of dead left unburied in their homes or in the streets, rotting in the brutal summer heat. The strict quarantine meant no one except relief workers was allowed in or out, trains sped through at high speed without stopping, and all contact with the outside world was lost. A reporter for the St. Louis *Globe Democrat* wrote, "Grenada, passed in the night, contained a single light illuminating the yellow face of a corpse lying on the railway platform," while the *Pascagoula Democrat Star* announced the sad news that "Grenada is no longer a city. It is a morgue."

Farther north, the picturesque town of Holly Springs also fell to yellow fever, in part as a result of its citizens' desire to help other afflicted communities. In 1878 the cause of the fever was unknown. While it was common knowledge that the first frost usually put an end to outbreaks of yellow fever, people did not understand why. One theory held that the disease was caused by "bad air" in hot, humid lowland areas. An 1878 article in the *Holly Springs Reporter* noted, "The highest medical authorities say yellow fever cannot originate or spread at any altitude over 500 feet above sea level."

The residents of Holly Springs were so sure of the safety provided by the town's rolling hills that they refused to turn away refugees from infected areas. A letter from a citizen of Grenada to his "Uncle Jack" in Holly Springs noted, "I was much pleased with the invitation of your townsmen inviting citizens of Grenada and other places to come and take shelter in your healthy city. It is so unlike the selfishness displayed by most places, that I continually pray that your place may not be visited by the yellow scourge." Unfortunately, it was a prayer that went unanswered. The fever followed refugees to Holly Springs, claiming

more lives in the town than the Civil War. In September of 1878 the
chairman of the Holly Springs Relief Committee wrote, "The hospital
is full, and it looks like every man must go down. Only ten out of the
first 100 cases live. . . . Five hundred persons now lie stricken. We pray
for friends and frost."

Yellow jack also took over Port Gibson. The town newspaper, the
Port Gibson Reveille, suspended publication during the epidemic following the death of the printer. The first edition of the paper released after
the plague noted, "It would be impossible to describe the pestilence
when in the height of its fury . . . utter silence reigned in our streets.
Every home was a hospital. The dying and the dead were all around.
Corpses, just as the victims died, wrapped in sheets and blankets and
hurriedly encoffined, were stealthily lifted out of doors, and sometimes
out of windows, and buried in haste at sunrise, after dark, by dim lanterns, and frequently lay all night long in the graveyard unburied."

Conditions were equally grisly in Greenwood. A report from that
city in the Mississippi Delta noted, "There was not a casket left, so they
commandeered lumber, and men made plain, unpainted wooden boxes,
which served for rich and poor, black and white alike. No longer could
the question of family plot in the cemetery be considered. Instead, there
were mass graves dug in long rows to stand ready as the victims fell."

The epidemic of 1878 also afflicted African Americans, who were
previously thought to be immune to the disease. John Prestridge Freeman, a resident of rural Newton County, who lost four members of
his family to the disease, noted that yellow fever, at least temporarily,
took precedence over issues of black and white. "The sad task of burying the dead was, of necessity, entrusted to the Negroes, since the few
white men who were not sick must devote their efforts for the sick and
dying," Freeman wrote. "Let it be said to the eternal praise of these
black men, that not one person, white or colored, lacked a reverent,
dignified burial as time and circumstance would permit. Not one grave

was left unmarked, which alone made it possible for survivors to find the resting places of loved ones later. These Negroes, who had been slaves such a short time before, displayed a loyalty and devotion that was monumental."

More than sixty cities and communities in Mississippi fell victim to the epidemic between May and November of 1878, posting death tolls ranging from one to more than one thousand people. Hardest hit was Vicksburg, which reported nearly 6,000 cases and 1,500 deaths. Still recovering from a brutal Civil War siege, Vicksburg now faced a new terror in the form of yellow jack. As one resident wrote, "We have seen the horrors of the battlefield . . . but we have never witnessed anything that so awakened the sensibilities of our nature."

Contributing to the statewide terror was the mystery as to what caused the disease and the complete lack of any preventative or cure. One doctor who survived the epidemic wrote later that yellow fever was "a mystery in nature, one of the hidden ways of God." Physicians were at a loss as to how to treat the disease; "treatments" like bleeding the patients had no effect on the disease and increased the suffering of its victims. As the editor of the *Jackson Daily Bulletin* noted, "Dr. Jack Frost is the only yellow fever expert in whom the people have absolute confidence."

The epidemic of 1878 not only took human lives, but also killed commerce. Every outbreak sent panic throughout the entire United States. Putting cities under quarantine meant closing ports, stopping trains in their tracks, and shutting down all forms of trade. Quarantine regulations called for the fumigation of mail, and the shipping of potentially infected cotton was forbidden. The few businesses that did remain open demanded cash payment, suspending all forms of credit out of fear that their customers would not live long enough to pay their bills.

In some cases yellow fever killed entire towns, both in terms of their people and their economies. Beechland, a once-thriving town near Vicksburg, completely disappeared as a result of the 1878 epidemic; all that remains today is a lichen-covered monument reading, "In memory of my entire family."

The entire industrial development of Mississippi and the South was crippled. A letter to the *Washington Post* dated September 9, 1878, and signed by officials in Mississippi, Alabama, and Louisiana described the economic chaos created by the fever. "In New Orleans, Vicksburg, and Memphis, as well as the smaller towns of Holly Springs, Grenada, Port Gibson, Canton, and Greenville . . . all business is entirely suspended. [Unemployed men] have no means to get away from the pest-ridden cities; for them there is no labor, no wages, no bread—nothing but death or starvation . . ." The cost of the epidemic to Mississippi, a state already adversely affected by the Civil War, was estimated at $40 million.

By late September of 1878 conditions in Mississippi had become so dire that Governor John M. Stone made a proclamation, pleading, "that on Friday, the 30th day of September, all Christian people throughout the State repair to their respective places of worship and offer up their united petition in prayer to God, that He will withdraw from our people this terrible affliction, and that He, in His infinite goodness and mercy, will restore them to health and bring peace to their mourning households."

The yellow fever epidemic ended in the fall, with the arrival of the frost. The last death was reported on November 28, 1878, in Jackson, and days later, the Mississippi Board of Health, an organization created in response to yellow fever, declared the epidemic over. Throughout the late fall and early winter, quarantines were lifted and boats and trains returned refugees to their hometowns. Schools and businesses reopened, and churches used as hospitals were restored as places of worship. By January of 1879 Mississippi was cautiously looking toward an economic and business recovery.

Two fear-filled decades would pass before researchers discovered that yellow fever was borne by mosquitoes. By 1900 organized efforts to control the mosquito population in cities and states throughout the South prevented yellow fever from ever again spreading to such epidemic proportions. In 1951 Harvard scientist Max Thieler won the Nobel Prize in Medicine for his development of a yellow fever vaccine.

If there could be such a thing as a "bright side" to the yellow fever epidemic of 1878, it would be that the same fever that brought so much death to the South also brought healing to the nation. The United States was still recovering from the animosity of the Civil War when the epidemic broke out. Horrified by reports coming from the southern states, residents of the northern states sent money, supplies, and medical professionals to assist their stricken countrymen. Former Union General George B. McClellan, by then the governor of New Jersey, called the citizens of his state to provide offerings for "the relief of our unfortunate fellow citizens of the afflicted districts of the South . . . fellow citizens once arrayed in arms against us, but now, through God's mercy, happily reunited with us."

"The terrors of war in the spring of 1863 scarcely equaled the ravages of the yellow fever in the summer and fall of 1878," an account from a resident in Port Gibson noted. "The response from the outside was prompt and liberal. Nurses were employed from a distance. Immense sums of money were sent from northern cities, villages, churches, and individuals." The flood of financial, material, and spiritual aid from North to South overshadowed national antagonism.

Father Abram Ryan was a former Confederate chaplain and a renowned poet dedicated to memorializing the South and its "lost cause." According to Edward Blum in the *Journal of Southern History*, "Ryan's feelings toward northerners and toward the Union changed considerably after a devastating yellow fever outbreak in 1878 ravaged much of the South and was met by a massive relief effort on the part of northern whites." After the epidemic, Abram penned a poem titled, "Reunited."

For at the touch of Mercy's hand
The North and South stood side by side . . .

Thou givest back my sons again,
The Southland to the Northland cries. . . .

I still my sobs, I cease my tears,
Thou hast recompensed my anguished years.

Jefferson Davis, the former president of the Confederate States of America, lost his adult son to the epidemic. Davis, who had only recently been released from prison for his role in the conflict between North and South, wrote a letter of thanks to all northerners who had offered aid during the epidemic, noting that, "The noble generosity of the northern people in this day of our extreme affliction has been felt with deep gratitude and has done more for the fraternization of North and South than many volumes of rhetorical assurance."

The yellow fever epidemic of 1878 also led to organized public health efforts at the national and state levels, including the founding of a National Board of Health and of the Mississippi State Board of Health, both of which were motivated by the realization that an organized approach was needed to combat contagions like yellow fever.

In a report to Congress Dr. John Woodworth, the national Marine Hospital Service surgeon general, emphasized the importance of united, organized efforts to battle yellow jack, saying, "Yellow fever should be dealt with as an enemy which imperils life and cripples commerce and industry. To no other great nation of the earth is yellow fever so calamitous as to the United States of America."

BIEDENHARN GIVES
THE WORLD A COKE

1894

There are few places in the world in which one cannot purchase a Coca-Cola. Coke is one of the most recognized and beloved brands and most widely distributed products on the planet, thanks in part to the bright idea of a twenty-eight-year-old candy store owner in Vicksburg.

Coca-Cola was invented in 1886 by Dr. John Pemberton, an Atlanta pharmacist who first brewed up the now-classic beverage in his backyard. Pemberton's bookkeeper suggested the name "Coca-Cola," a nod to the new drink's chief ingredients. Originally marketed as a "healthful tonic," the original formula contained extracts of cocaine as well as the caffeine-rich kola nut.

Pemberton began selling his new beverage at the local drugstore, Jacob's Pharmacy, where customers were more than willing to shell out five cents a glass for his delicious new concoction. In his first year of business, Pemberton sold an impressive average of nine glasses of Coca-Cola a day.

In 1887 another Atlanta pharmacist, Asa Candler, secured the rights to Coca-Cola for $2,300. Candler was a savvy businessman who had a knack for promotions. By the mid-1890s Candler's aggressive marketing of Coca-Cola had made it one of America's most popular soda fountain drinks. Candler had built a successful business selling the secret formula syrup to soda fountain proprietors, who added carbonated water to the syrup to create the popular beverage.

One of Coca-Cola's early "sales reps" was Joseph "Joe" Biedenharn, a candy store owner in Vicksburg. As a young man, Biedenharn went to work in the family business, a confectionary shop called Biedenharn & Brothers founded by his father and uncle. Joe Biedenharn gradually took over the business, renaming it the Biedenharn Candy Company.

A shrewd businessman who recognized a good thing when he tasted it, Biedenharn sold Coca-Cola to retail customers at the soda fountain in his candy store and also sold the Coca-Cola syrup wholesale to other soda fountains in the Vicksburg area. As he made his rounds to wholesale customers in outlying areas by wagon, he also filled their orders for bottled soda water. Biedenharn originally relied on a local bottler to supply him with the soda water, but finding his source to be unreliable, he eventually opened his own soda water bottling plant, bottling and selling lemon, strawberry, and sarsaparilla soda water.

As the demand for Coca-Cola at the local soda fountains grew, Biedenharn was struck with an idea—why not bottle Coca-Cola? That way, he reasoned, the "country folk" who did not have easy access to a city soda fountain could also enjoy the popular soft drink. With the necessary syrup, equipment, gas, bottles, and crates on hand, it was only a matter of moments before Biedenharn was holding the world's first bottled Coke—a simple concept that would travel from Vicksburg around the world.

In a letter to Harrison Jones, vice president of the Coca-Cola Company, dated 1939, Biedenharn recalled:

> *It was in the summer of 1894 that we first bottled*
> *Coca-Cola [on] Washington Street in Vicksburg, Mis-*
> *sissippi. . . . Consumer demand had increased and was*
> *increasing rapidly, and as Coca-Cola could only be*
> *had in the cities where fountains were dispensing it,*
> *this thought struck one day—why not bottle it for our*
> *country trade? We were in the soda water bottling game*
> *and it was easy to start it going. We sent one of our*
> *first cases of bottled Coca-Cola to Mr. Candler, and he*
> *wrote back that it was fine.*

Biedenharn's price for a case of bottled Coca-Cola was seventy cents, compared to sixty cents per case for plain soda water.

"The other soda water bottlers didn't want to bother with it," Biedenharn said in an interview with *The Coca-Cola Bottler* magazine some fifty years after he put the cap on the first bottle of Coke. "They said the price for Coca-Cola was too high. But I saw the demand for Coca-Cola in town and I thought it would be profitable in the country if I could only get it there. I found the more Coca-Cola I was able to sell, the more I made out of it."

When Asa Candler saw how well Biedenharn was doing with sales of bottled Coke, he gave Biedenharn the entire state of Mississippi as an exclusive sales territory. In 1899, perhaps underestimating the potential of bottling the product, Candler sold the bottling rights to Coca-Cola to two Chattanooga lawyers for the sum of one dollar. Candler left the Mississippi territory belonging to Biedenharn out of that contract, ensuring that the soft drink's original bottler would still reap the rewards of his simple yet brilliant idea.

The Chattanooga pioneer bottlers divided the United States into territories and sold bottling rights to local entrepreneurs; Biedenharn himself purchased territories in Louisiana, Arkansas, and Texas. As the 1920s dawned, more than a thousand Coca-Cola bottlers were operating in the United States. By the close of the decade, bottle sales of Coca-Cola exceeded fountain sales.

Over the years, bottled Coca-Cola became the key to the company's global success. Once the product was "portable" and accessible worldwide, everyone had to have a taste of the real thing. Packaging, from the distinctive, contoured bottle specifically designed to be "recognizable in the dark" to six-packs for easy transport to open-top coolers, made it easier for people to enjoy Coca-Cola at home or on the go and helped make Coke a worldwide sensation.

Today, Coca-Cola products are available in more than two hundred countries. And if Dr. Pemberton was pleased to see his beverage sell nine servings a day at the local soda fountain, one can only imagine his reaction if he could see that today Coca-Cola sells more than 1.7 billion servings a day.

Joseph Biedenharn, the entrepreneur who helped take Coca-Cola from the soda fountain to the world, went on to become the president of The Coca-Cola Bottling Company of Monroe, Louisiana. Biedenharn's three sons followed him into the Coca-Cola bottling business, as did several of Biedenharn's brothers and nephews. He died in 1952, still proud of his title as the original Coca-Cola bottler.

Biedenharn's story lives on in the Biedenharn Coca-Cola Museum in Vicksburg. Located in the original building that once housed the Biedenharn Candy Company and was the site of the first bottling of Coca-Cola, the museum is filled with exhibits on the history of Coca-Cola and the Biedenharn family. The Biedenharns bottled Coca-Cola here and in other locations in downtown Vicksburg until 1938, when a new Coca-Cola bottling plant was built in Vicksburg. The building was sold and used for a variety of commercial purposes until 1979, when the Biedenharn family repurchased the building and converted it into a museum. The family then donated the building to the Vicksburg Foundation for Historic Preservation. Displays include a reproduction of the equipment first used to bottle Coca-Cola and Coca-Cola memorabilia from past to present. Restored to its original 1890 appearance, the candy store offers ice cream, fountain Cokes, and old-fashioned Coke floats—a fitting tribute to Joseph Biedenharn, the entrepreneur who helped give the world a Coke.

THE BIRTH OF THE BLUES

1895

The Mississippi Delta blues is a combination of mournful wails and dryly humorous, often bawdy lyrics that's every bit a way of life as much as a musical form.

The blues was born from the chants of slaves who worked the cotton fields of Mississippi prior to the Civil War, and often continued to work those same fields as sharecroppers long after the battles ended. The blues began as an elaboration on work chants, slave "sorrow songs," and the lyrical, haunting "field hollers" of one laborer to another that echoed across the cotton fields. The music included tones from the music of Africa and reflected the nuances of the many tribes whose members were enslaved in the American South.

From these humble beginnings, the blues went on to influence every other form of American music. Polished and transplanted to nightclubs in Chicago, urbanized blues became jazz, and another Mississippi native, Elvis Presley, combined the blues with country music to give the world rock 'n' roll. The repertoire of any blues or rock band is full of songs, guitar licks, and vocal inflections borrowed from Mississippi bluesmen, and virtually every song heard on the radio today, from jazz to country to rock 'n' roll to hip hop to rap, has its roots in the Mississippi Delta blues.

Widely recognized as America's only original music, the blues and its Mississippi birthplace are synonymous to music lovers. But while there is no doubt the blues was born in Mississippi, its actual birth date and birthplace are impossible to confirm.

Dockery Farms, however, can stake a strong claim to being the spot where the music took its first bluesy breath. Located on Mississippi Highway 8 between the small Delta communities of Cleveland and Ruleville, Dockery Farms was founded in 1895 by Will Dockery, who began a cotton plantation on the forty-square-mile property's rich soil. Dockery's reputation for treating his workers and sharecroppers fairly attracted a large number of black laborers; eventually more than four hundred tenant families and two thousand workers found their way to this isolated plantation. At its peak, Dockery Farms was essentially a self-sufficient town with an elementary school, churches, post office, resident doctor, railroad depot, ferry, blacksmith shop, cotton gin, cemeteries, picnic grounds, and a commissary that sold dry goods, furniture, and groceries. The workers were even paid in Dockery Farms' own currency.

The workers' quarters included boardinghouses where they lived, socialized, and spent a great deal of their leisure time playing music, accompanying themselves on guitars, banjos, harmonicas, and jugs. Initially, the musicians played for their own enjoyment. Writing and playing original songs was a form of personal expression, as well as a welcome diversion from their hard lives of labor.

Around 1900 sharecroppers Bill and Annie Patton moved to Dockery Farms with their nine-year-old son, Charley. Taught and influenced by an older musician on the farm named Henry Sloan, Charley Patton soon earned a reputation as a masterful musician. By

1910 Patton was influencing other bluesmen. They included his longtime partner Willie Brown; Tommy Johnson, who became the most influential musician in the Jackson area; Howlin' Wolf, who took guitar lessons from Patton after moving to the area as a teen; and Roebuck "Pops" Staples, who later led the gospel group the Staple Singers.

Thanks to Patton and the other bluesmen, Dockery Farms soon became known as *the* place for the area's black population to come and enjoy the blues, music that was uniquely their own. Patton's nephew, Tom Cannon, recalled an outdoor concert at Dockery Plantation attended by hundreds of blues fans that featured his uncle as the star attraction. "On a Saturday a whole bunch would get together, and he'd play at Dockery's at the big brick store. He'd sit out there on the store porch. People [came] from Lula, Cleveland, everywhere. . . . They would charge so much at the door."

Patton and the other bluesmen also performed around the Delta at dances, fish fries, and house parties, becoming popular with white as well as black audiences. The musicians made about twenty-five dollars for a performance at a party—approximately five or ten times what they could earn picking crops in the field. In addition to freedom from the backbreaking work, the blues won the men celebrity and legions of adoring female fans.

Patton's music might never have been recorded had it not been for H. C. Speir, a Jackson music store owner who traveled to Dockery Farms to see Patton perform. Impressed by what he heard, Speir arranged for Patton to record. In 1929 Patton recorded fourteen songs for Paramount Records. They immediately became top sellers, leading to his second recording session for the ARC company in New York in 1934.

Many of the songs Patton recorded addressed daily life and events in the Delta, including some at Dockery. In "34 Blues" Patton sang of being banished from Dockery by plantation manager Herman Jett—the lyric lamented "they run me from Will Dockery's" —apparently because Patton was running off with various tenants' women. Patton's "Pea Vine Blues" referred to a train line that ran from Dockery westward through the Delta.

Thanks to the record labels the blues soon found an audience outside the South. By the mid-1920s record companies were combing the Mississippi Delta, auditioning every black man they could find who could play the guitar, and giving the promising ones train tickets north to record. Soon they hastened the process by sending the recording equipment South, setting up makeshift studios in hotel rooms.

With the onset of the Depression, the record companies cut back, recording only proven acts, but the bluesmen of the Delta continued to perform. On weekends in the 1920s and 1930s, bluesmen traveled to Mississippi Delta towns to shop and socialize, and to play their unique music on street corners and in rough-and-tumble nightclubs called "juke joints." In these makeshift social clubs, songs and lyrics were borrowed and techniques and styles were enhanced. Young bluesmen found mentors and left home to follow them on the road. From Mississippi the bluesmen headed north to Chicago, where they amplified their instruments, added drums and horns, and went from single bluesman to blues bands.

But most of the later blues greats, including the legendary B. B. King and McKinley Morganfield, better known as Muddy Waters, still hailed from Mississippi. Within decades that simple music from the cotton fields would change the sound of music worldwide. Musicians, including Eric Clapton, Robert Plant of Led Zeppelin, and the members of ZZ Top, credited Muddy Waters as the primary influence on their music. Clapton once said, "Muddy took the music of the Delta plantation, transplanted it in a Chicago nightclub, surrounded it with an electric band, and changed the course of popular music forever."

Back in Mississippi, Charley Patton's relatives continued to live and work at Dockery, and though he roamed the Delta and beyond performing, Dockery Farms remained Patton's most frequent stopping point until his death in 1934. In 1936 Will Dockery's son, Joe Rice Dockery, inherited Dockery Farms. As workers traded life in the agricultural South for industrial jobs in urban areas, the large, self-sufficient plantation communities gradually died out.

Initially, Dockery Farms' owners had paid little attention to the groundbreaking music born on their land. "We were never the type of plantation owners who invited their help to come in and sing for parties," Keith Dockery, Joe Rice Dockery's widow, would say years later. "I wish we had realized that these people were so important." In later years the Dockery family took great pride in the role their property had played in birthing America's only original music. Later generations of the Dockery family established the Dockery Farm Foundation to preserve the plantation site and support research on the Mississippi Delta blues. In 2006 the property was added to the National Register of Historic Places.

Dockery Plantation may claim to be the blues' birthplace, but the entire Mississippi Delta was its cradle. Today, Mississippi is a Mecca for thousands of music lovers from around the word who come to explore the haunts of the old bluesmen. Many blues fans follow the Mississippi Blues Trail, a series of historical markers that combine words and images to tell the story of the music, from its blues-tinted past to the living blues of today and the next generation of blues in the making. Markers recounting the lives of bluesmen and women and explaining how the land where they lived and the struggles they faced influenced their music are found throughout Mississippi. Markers stand guard over neon-lit streets and dusty back roads, quiet cotton fields and rowdy juke joints, over peaceful churches where the gospel saves souls and dark crossroads where the devil offers to buy them. A project of the Mississippi Blues Commission, the Mississippi Blues Trail represents the combined work of the world's foremost blues scholars and historians.

The entire Mississippi Delta is dotted with blues museums, murals, and ramshackle old buildings where an art form was born, musical history was made, and the pain and weariness of hard labor inspired America's only original music.

THE FIRST TEDDY BEAR

1902

A presidential pardon issued in the tiny town of Onward led to the creation of one of the world's most enduring toys.

In November of 1902 President Theodore Roosevelt traveled to Mississippi to resolve a boundary dispute between the states of Mississippi and Louisiana. A skilled outdoorsman and avid big game hunter, Roosevelt combined his tour of the area with a five-day black bear hunt. Holt Collier, a former slave, Confederate solder, and skilled hunting guide widely regarded as the greatest bear hunter in the South, led the expedition into the Mississippi Delta.

The reporters covering the president's tour soon lost interest in the boundary dispute, focusing their coverage instead on Roosevelt's failure to kill a trophy black bear. The final day of the hunt found the hunting party near the small Delta community of Onward. When a 235-pound black bear attacked one of Collier's prized hunting dogs, the guide clubbed and lassoed the bear, tied it to a tree, and invited the president to shoot it. Roosevelt refused to kill the tethered animal, pointing out that it would not be sportsmanlike to shoot a captive bear. Following the president's orders, Collier cut the rope and released the bear.

Clifford Berryman, a cartoonist with the *Washington Post,* heard of President Roosevelt's noble deed. Berryman penned a cartoon depicting the president turning his back on a cowering, captured bear cub with a caption reading, "Drawing the line in Mississippi." As newspapers nationwide picked up the cartoon, the story of "Teddy's bear" quickly spread, generating tremendous positive response, along with the persistent and mistaken impression that the bear had been a cub.

Soon after, a New York candy and sundry shop owner named Morris Michtom and his wife Rose made toy history by creating a stuffed, cuddly toy they christened "Teddy's bear." The first bear was hand-sewn by Rose Michtom and placed in the shop window as a display model, where it immediately created a sensation.

Concerned that they might offend the president by using his name without permission, the Michtoms mailed the original bear to the White House, offering it as a gift for the president's children and asking President Roosevelt for permission to name their new line of toy bears in his honor.

Roosevelt replied, writing, "I warmly thank you for your letter and the fine stuffed bear you made. I can hardly wait to show my children. I don't think my name is likely to be worth much in the toy bear business, but you are welcome to use it."

Roosevelt was mistaken. The Michtoms' "Teddy's bears," later shortened to "Teddy bears," were a phenomenal success. Demand was so great that the Michtoms soon dedicated themselves to producing the bears full time. In 1903 Michtom, who had arrived in America from Russia as a penniless immigrant less than twenty years earlier, founded the Ideal Novelty and Toy Company, later known as the Ideal Toy Company, starting the entire business with revenues generated by the original teddy bear.

Recognizing the teddy bear's charm and national popularity, Theodore Roosevelt and the Republican Party adopted the bear as their symbol in the election of 1904. Michtom bears were placed on display at every public White House function. The original teddy bear, treasured and saved by Teddy Roosevelt's grandchildren, is now displayed at the Smithsonian.

Holt Collier, the great hunter who led the expedition, went on to kill a reported three thousand bears in his lifetime—more than Daniel Boone and Davy Crockett combined. In 1907 he led Roosevelt on another black bear hunt in Louisiana, but the successes of that hunt were overshadowed by the "failure" of the first. President Roosevelt went on to call Collier, "the greatest hunter and guide I have ever known." In recognition of Collier's extraordinary wilderness skills, Mississippi's Holt Collier National Wildlife Refuge—one of seven refuges in the state's Theodore Roosevelt National Wildlife Refuge Complex—was named in his honor.

More than a century after the great hunt that inspired a national icon, Onward remains a sleepy little community. The Onward Store in town displays photographs from Roosevelt's famous bear hunt and sells souvenir teddy bears. In a final footnote—or "pawnote"—to the story, in 2002 the Mississippi legislature passed a bill recognizing the teddy bear as the official state toy of Mississippi.

THE WITCH OF
YAZOO

1904

At first glance Yazoo City is just a quiet little town tucked between the rolling hills of north Mississippi and the flat edge of the Mississippi Delta. But in addition to a hilly side and a delta side, Yazoo City boasts a dark side. The town is home to the final resting place of the dreaded Witch of Yazoo.

The witch's tale has been handed down through generations, a scary story used to convince naughty children to behave. Late Mississippi author Willie Morris immortalized the legend of the Witch of Yazoo in his book of childhood reminiscences, *Good Old Boy,* and the witch's story hit the silver screen in the Hollywood version of Morris's book, *My Dog Skip.*

As the legend holds, in the late 1800s Yazoo City was home to a self-proclaimed witch, a crazy, cackling old woman who lured unsuspecting fishermen to their deaths in her dark shack on the banks of the Yazoo River. After burying their bodies, it was whispered, the evil witch danced on their graves.

As Morris recounted in *Good Old Boy:*

> *One late afternoon in the autumn of 1884, a boy*
> *named Joe Bob Duggett was passing by her house on a*
> *raft when he heard a terrible, ungodly moan from one*
> *of the rooms. He tied his raft to a cypress branch, ran*
> *to the house, and looked through a window. What he*
> *saw chilled his blood and bones. Two dead men were*
> *stretched out on the floor of the parlor, and the old*
> *woman, wearing a black dress caked with filth and*
> *cockleburs, had turned her face up to the ceiling and*
> *was singing some dreadful incantations, waving her*
> *arms in demented circles all the while.*
>
> *Joe Bob Duggett raced to his raft, floated into*
> *town, and told the sheriff and his men what he had*
> *seen. They got a horse and buggy and sped to the old*
> *woman's house. . . . They smashed down the front door,*
> *but were unable to find either the dead men (who*
> *have never been found to this day) or the demented old*
> *woman. They climbed the stairs to the attic, opened the*
> *door an inch or two, and caught sight of several dozen*
> *half-starved cats, all bunched together and gyrating in*
> *their wild insanity. Two skeletons, which were never*
> *identified by the sheriff's office, dangled from a dusty*
> *rafter. Fish bones littered the floor, and the smell was*
> *unusually pungent. The sheriff, his deputies, and Joe*
> *Bob stood there transfixed, finally banging the door shut*
> *when eight or ten of the cats tried to get out.*

The old woman tried to sneak out the back door of the shack,
but the sheriff and his men chased her into a nearby swamp, where

she met her death in a pool of quicksand. Just before her "ghastly, pockmarked head" was sucked below the surface, she vowed to return from the grave and burn the entire town to the ground on May 25.

The men used pitchforks to retrieve the old woman's body from its sandy grave and buried it in Glenwood Cemetery. They surrounded her plot with a thick, iron chain. "If she can break through that and burn down Yazoo," the sheriff said, "she deserves to burn it down."

Call it a witch's curse or an ironic twist of fate, but twenty years later, on May 25, 1904, all of downtown Yazoo City was consumed by a raging fire. According to Morris,

> *Many fine homes were destroyed, and every bank, every physician's, lawyer's and dentist's office, every hotel and boardinghouse, every meat market and bakery, the newspaper and printing office, every church, clubroom, and lodge room, every telephone, telegraph and express office, the depot, the post office, every furniture store, every hardware store, all but one livery stable, all but one drugstore, every barbershop, every tailor shop, every undertaking establishment, and, in fact, nearly every business necessity.*

The next day, as the flames still smoldered, the town elders made a visit to the witch's grave.

"What they discovered would be passed along to my friends and to me many years later, and as boys we would go see it for ourselves, for no repairs were made, as a reminder to future generations," Morris wrote. "As if by some supernatural strength, the chain around the grave had been broken in two."

How much of the witch's legend is true and how much is folklore remains a mystery, but one thing is certain—the witch's grave is still there in Glenwood Cemetery, and the chain around it is still missing a link. Decades after the fire of 1904, a tall marker was erected adjacent to the original witch's grave that read, "According to local legend . . . on May 25, 1904, the Witch of Yazoo City broke out of these curious chain links surrounding her grave and burned down Yazoo City. Writer Willie Morris' *Good Old Boy* brought national renown to this vengeful woman and her shameful deed." When Willie Morris died, he was buried in Glenwood Cemetery, thirteen paces from the witch's grave.

THE GREAT
MISSISSIPPI RIVER FLOOD

1927

"Mississippi" is Choctaw for "Father of Waters," referring to the mighty river for which the state is named. From the land's earliest days, the river was a source of commerce and transportation, and its delta was home to the most fertile soil on earth. For those who lived along its banks, the river was a life-sustaining force.

But in the spring of 1927, the Father of Waters proved it could also be a deadly force. In what remains the most destructive river flood in US history, the great river overflowed its banks and overpowered the levees designed to tame it, drowning more than sixteen million acres in seven states, killing at least 500 people, and displacing 600,000 more.

In Mississippi alone, 200,000 people were left homeless. More than 77,000 homes were flooded, damaged, or destroyed, along with hundreds of public buildings. Tens of thousands of animals, including dogs, cats, cattle, hogs, chickens, work animals, and wildlife were drowned, and an entire year's crop was lost as the country's richest farmland sat underwater for four devastating months.

The flood began in the winter and early spring of 1927, when rain drenched the central basin of the Mississippi in biblical proportions, exceeding the annual average by as much as ten inches. Tributaries of the Mississippi River north of the state of Mississippi overflowed their banks, causing floods in Oklahoma, Kansas, Illinois, and Kentucky.

By April 15, 1927—Good Friday—the danger was flowing south. The Memphis *Commercial Appeal* warned, "The roaring Mississippi River, from St. Louis to New Orleans, is believed to be on its mightiest rampage. . . . All along the Mississippi, considerable fear is felt over the prospects for the greatest flood in history."

That Good Friday morning more record-breaking rains came, pounding most of the states of Missouri, Illinois, Arkansas, Mississippi, Texas, and Louisiana. The river swelled so high and flowed so fast that for the residents of cities along its banks, "It was like facing an angry, dark ocean."

The US Army Corps of Engineers assured the public that the levee system designed to confine and channel the river into the Gulf of Mexico would hold. Of particular concern was the Mounds Landing levee just north of Greenville. A crevasse—a break in the levee—at Mounds Landing would flood the city of 15,000 and allow water to engulf the valuable farmland of the Mississippi Delta.

Men known as "levee guards" were placed in camps at critical sites along the top of the levee. As the water rose, the men filled and stacked thousands of sandbags, struggling to stay ahead of the rising water. For days, trucks raced back and forth through Greenville day and night, hauling more sand and more men. Every able-bodied man was rounded up to help. Convicts were pulled from the local jails and transported to the levee; patrols ran through black neighborhoods and grabbed men off the street to send them to the waterfront. If a black man refused, he was beaten or jailed; more than one man was shot.

But in the battle of man versus the Mississippi River, the river was the victor. By daybreak on April 21, 1927, five hundred men had worked through the night in driving rain and forty-degree temperatures in a futile effort to save the levee, but the river was rising too fast. Moses Mason, one of the five hundred piling sandbags on the levee, recalled, "The levee felt like jelly. The water was boiling up. The levee just started shaking. You could feel it shaking." Fifteen hundred more men were rushed to the levee to no avail. The sandbags began to float away as soon as they were tossed. Water began leaking through small breaches in the levee, as well as over the top. Then someone shouted, "Run for your lives! It's gonna break!"

Just after 7:00 a.m., the Mississippi River crashed through the levee at Mounds Landing in a 100-foot channel half a mile wide. Water poured through the crevasse in amounts double that of Niagara Falls. As the levee collapsed, hundreds of the workers were swept away, many to their deaths.

Army district engineer Major John Lee wired the head of the Army Corps of Engineers, "Levee broke at ferry landing Mounds, Mississippi eight a.m. Crevasse will overflow the entire Mississippi Delta." A man named John Hall was covering the phones in the levee board office in Greenville. When word came to him of the crevasse, he broke the news to chief engineer Seguine Allen. "I took him the message," Hall said, "and the old man just sat there and cried."

While engineers had realized Mounds Landing was a vulnerable point, nothing could have prepared them for a disaster of this magnitude. The crevasse widened until a muddy tidal wave three-quarters of a mile across and 100 feet high swept through the Delta, swallowing everything in its path. The water's force carved a 100-foot-deep channel half a mile wide stretching a mile inland. Within ten days of the levee break at Mounds Landing, one million acres of valuable farmland was ten feet underwater.

Fire whistles screamed in Greenwood, signaling LeFlore County's 185,000 residents that the levee had failed. The frightened citizens began evacuating, packing automobiles, trains, and wagons in a frantic effort to outrun the flood. Sixty miles east and ninety miles south of the crevasse, there was nothing but water. Trees, farms, homes, and businesses were washed away in seconds. Dead people and animals floated aside debris in the muddy water.

Thousands of people stranded in trees or on rooftops prayed for help to come before their precarious positions went under or were washed away. Water wasn't the only danger; dozens of drenched townspeople who survived drowning died from exposure as they waited in the rain and cold for rescue that never came.

Every canoe, raft, and boat in the area was pressed into service. Hundreds of flood victims were saved by commercial fishermen from the Mississippi Gulf Coast, who put their boats on trains and unloaded them on the edge of the floodwaters, and by bootleggers from nearby Arkansas, who brought their fastest boats to aid in the rescue. Many rescuers were forced to use guns to keep the panicked victims from swamping and capsizing the boats sent to save them.

William Alexander Percy, chairman of the Greenville Relief Committee, later wrote in his autobiography, *Lanterns on the Levee,*

> *For thirty-six hours, the Delta was in turmoil, in movement, in terror. Then the waters covered everything, the turmoil ceased, and a great quiet settled down. . . . Over everything was silence, deadlier because of the strange cold sound of the currents gnawing at foundations, hissing against walls, creaming and clawing over obstacles.*

The initial terror was followed by four miserable months of life in a flooded land. Hundreds of residents who did not evacuate were housed in a refugee camp on the levee, while other citizens navigated the streets of their city via boat, and later via raised wooden walkways over the fetid, filthy water.

Local officials called in the National Guard to keep order, while the Red Cross provided tents, food, and emergency supplies to the displaced citizens of Mississippi and other states crippled by the flood. It was the greatest relief effort in the history of the Red Cross, carrying a final price tag of $17 million. In Mississippi alone, the Red Cross cared for 69,574 people in eighteen refugee camps and provided food for more than 72,000 surviving animals.

The great flood also led to the greatest racial conflict since the Civil War. Yielding to pressure from wealthy white landowners who feared that if the black workers left Mississippi, they would never return and the cost of labor would rise, the National Guard refused to allow black men to evacuate. Instead, they were rounded up into what amounted to concentration camps along the levee. Here they lived in tents and worked in deplorable conditions, filling, hauling, and stacking sand bags from sunup until sundown for seventy-five cents per day, or as the weeks dragged on, for no pay at all. Some were also put to work distributing Red Cross food packages, which were coming in by the barge full. They received no pay for the relief work but were instead told that if they did not work, they would not receive their share of Red Cross rations.

The tented work camp stretched along the Greenville levee for seven miles, a malodorous, muddy, squalid, wretched scene marked by too many men living on a thin sliver of dry ground, sharing too few tents, fighting over too little food, and worked to the point of exhaustion. Any black man who tried to leave the work camp was driven back to his station at gunpoint by the National Guard.

Word of the mistreatment of the blacks in the levee camps reached Secretary of Commerce Herbert Hoover, who served as chairman of a national committee formed to coordinate flood relief. Hoover created the Colored Advisory Committee to look into the allegations of mistreatment, but when the committee delivered its report, he declined to take any action.

As the weeks dragged by, it became clear that the Army Corps of Engineers had gravely underestimated the power of the mighty Mississippi and of the levee system to contain it. Over the course of the flood, the levees were breached in more than 145 places along the river, drowning 27,000 square miles in fast-flowing, muddy water. Five weeks after the levee collapsed, engineers surveying the crevasse at Mounds Landing measured waves as high as 12 feet and water deeper than 100 feet. The crevasse itself was three-quarters of a mile wide. South of Greenville at Vicksburg, the swollen river was eighty miles wide.

It would be July before the floodwaters began to recede in the Mississippi Delta. With the aid of large pumps, the waters were drained in Greenville in late June, and a celebratory parade was held on July 4. As the waters receded, the evacuees returned and began the laborious and messy process of cleaning up their mud-caked property and rebuilding their homes and lives.

The flood of 1927 had far-reaching consequences. Prior to the flood, control of the Mississippi River had been left up to state and local authorities. In 1928 Congress passed the National Flood Control Act, which gave the federal government responsibility for "managing" the Mississippi River, including the redesign of the levee system from engineering to management.

As a result of the mistreatment and deplorable living conditions created by the flood, hundreds of African Americas left Mississippi in search of better lives and working conditions in the North.

Perhaps most notably, the flood served as a reminder that man would never truly be able to control nature. The Great Mississippi River Flood of 1927 remained the greatest natural disaster in American history until 2005, when the title was usurped by Hurricane Katrina, another force of nature that chose Mississippi as one of its proving grounds.

THE SOUND AND THE FURY

1929

Considered by many critics to be the greatest writer in American literary history, William Faulkner described Oxford and surrounding Lafayette County as his "little postage stamp of native soil." The region served as the inspiration for his novels of the glory and decline of the South, masterpieces of literature that earned Faulkner the Nobel and Pulitzer Prizes and made his works a staple in literature classes worldwide.

During his lifetime, Faulkner published nineteen novels, as well as dozens of short stories and poems. A complex man who shunned the limelight, Faulkner's reputation is larger than life. Once when asked to provide a biography to accompany a published short story, Faulkner sent back a brief, tongue-in-cheek paragraph concluding with, "own and operate [my] own typewriter."

Faulkner was born in 1897 in New Albany, a small town in northern Mississippi, and moved to Oxford with his family as a child. He was named after his great-grandfather, a colorful man who had also been a writer and who was killed in a duel before his namesake was born. Faulkner demonstrated artistic talent as a child and excelled academically in elementary school, but the confines of formal education soon bored him. He dropped out of high school after the eleventh grade.

With the outbreak of World War I, Faulkner attempted to enlist in the US Air Force, but at five feet, six inches tall, he was disqualified due to his height. Instead, Faulkner joined the Royal Air Force in Canada, lying about his birthplace and changing the family spelling of his name from "Falkner" to "Faulkner" to appear British. The war ended before Faulkner completed his training. Upon returning to Oxford, Faulkner shared many of his adventures in the war with his neighbors, few of whom realized the exploits he described were fictional.

In 1919 Faulkner began classes at the University of Mississippi ("Ole Miss") in Oxford, enrolling through a program for war veterans since he did not have a high school diploma. While a student at Ole Miss, he published poems and short stories in the campus newspaper but again became bored with formal education, earning a D in English and withdrawing from the university after three semesters.

Over the next few years, the future literary giant worked at several odd jobs, including a brief and disastrous stint as the university postmaster. Faulkner was reportedly the worst postmaster in the history of the job, losing the mail or failing to deliver it because the job didn't interest him. When a postal inspector came to investigate, Faulkner resigned the position, explaining that he "didn't care to be at the beck and call of any fool who could afford a postage stamp."

In 1924 Faulkner's first book, a volume of poetry titled *The Marble Faun,* was published. He continued to publish poems and short stories in literary magazines and in 1926 published his first novel, *Soldiers' Pay,* followed by *Mosquitos.*

As he began work on his third novel, *Flags in the Dust,* later published as *Sartoris,* Faulkner turned to his native region, drawing upon local lore and geography and his own family's history to create the fictional settings and people of Yoknapatawpha County. Years later, Faulkner said, "Beginning with *Sartoris,* I discovered that my own little postage stamp of native soil was worth writing about and that I would never live long enough to exhaust it."

Faulkner followed with a fourth novel also set in Yoknapatawpha titled *The Sound and the Fury.* Published in 1929 when Faulkner was just thirty-two years old, the novel is widely regarded as Faulkner's most significant work, the masterpiece that launched his greatest period of artistic achievement and established him as a literary genius. *The Sound and the Fury* takes its title from a passage in Shakespeare's *MacBeth,* which reads:

Life's but a walking shadow, a poor player
That struts and frets his hour upon the stage
And then is heard no more. It is a tale
Told by an idiot, full of sound and fury,
Signifying nothing.

It was an apt title; *The Sound and the Fury* has often been described as a southern Shakespearean tragedy. Written in changing points of view and stream-of-consciousness, the complex novel tells the story of the deterioration of the Compson family through the eyes of the Compson sons, including the mentally impaired Benjy, and Dilsey, the Compson family's black servant. Former Southern aristocrats, the Compsons struggle to deal with the financial, moral, and social decline of their family and its reputation. The Modern Library publishing company ranked *The Sound and the Fury* sixth on its list of the one hundred best English language novels of the twentieth century.

The Sound and the Fury was not immediately commercially successful, but when Faulkner's *Sanctuary,* a graphic tale of rape and murder, was published in 1931 to brisk sales, *The Sound and the Fury* also became a commercial and critical success.

As his reputation as a novelist grew, Faulkner's personal life also blossomed. He married his childhood sweetheart, Estelle Oldham, and the couple moved into an antebellum home in Oxford that he christened "Rowan Oak." Here Faulkner transformed his native land into an allegory for universal tales of the heart, explorations of the best and worst deeds, thoughts, and dreams of mankind. More novels set in Yoknapatawpha followed, including *As I Lay Dying, Sanctuary, Light in August, Absalom! Absalom!* and *Intruder in the Dust.* Set between the Civil War and the Great Depression, the novels focus on the universal and timeless questions of honor versus greed and recurring themes of isolation, poverty, racism, and social decline.

In addition to his work as a novelist, Faulkner discovered a second profession as a screenwriter, living off and on in Hollywood during the 1930s and 1940s while he worked on nearly fifty screenplays, most notably *To Have and Have Not* and *The Big Sleep.* Hollywood director Howard Hawks once introduced Faulkner to Clark Gable. When Gable asked Faulkner which authors he recommended, he replied, "Hemingway, Cather, Mann, Dos Passos, and William Faulkner." Gable then inquired, "Oh, Mr. Faulkner, do you write?" to which Faulkner replied, "Yes, Mr. Gable. What do you do?"

But it was Oxford and Rowan Oak where Faulkner truly found his inspiration. During a struggle with writer's block in Hollywood, Faulkner told his boss at the studio he thought he could concentrate better at home. Thinking Faulkner meant his apartment in Hollywood, the boss suggested he go there to work. He was later surprised to discover that Faulkner had taken his advice—and returned to Oxford to work on the script at Rowan Oak.

In 1949 William Faulkner received the Nobel Prize for Literature. On December 10, 1950, in Stockholm, Sweden, he delivered an acceptance speech that has since been recognized as one of the greatest in the history of the Nobel Prize. Faulkner noted:

> . . . *the problems of the human heart in conflict with itself which alone can make good writing because only that is worth writing about, worth the agony and the sweat. [The writer of today must relearn] the old verities and truths of the heart, the old universal truths lacking which any story is ephemeral and doomed—love and honor and pity and pride and compassion and sacrifice. Until he does so . . . he writes not of love but of lust, of defeats in which nobody loses anything of value, of victories without hope and, worst of all, without pity or compassion. His griefs grieve on no universal bones, leaving no scars. He writes not of the heart, but of the glands. Until he relearns these things, he will write as though he stood among and watched the end of man.*

After accepting the Novel Prize, Faulkner went on to receive two National Book Awards, the French Legion of Honor Award, two Pulitzer Prizes, and the Gold Medal for Fiction awarded by the American Academy of Arts and Letters.

Recognized worldwide as a literary genius and celebrity author, Faulkner attended conferences and cultural events throughout the United States and abroad. He bought a second house in Charlottesville, Virginia, from which he declined John F. Kennedy's invitation to a White House dinner for Nobel Prize winners, explaining that, "one hundred miles was too far to go for supper."

But no matter where he traveled, Faulkner always considered "home" to be his beloved Oxford. In Mississippi in July of 1962, the great writer died of a heart attack. Faulkner is buried in St. Peter's

Cemetery. Faithful readers and aspiring writers still leave dog-eared paperbacks and the occasional bottle of bourbon on his grave.

Since Faulkner's time, the town of Oxford has attracted a number of writers, who perhaps hoped a little of the Yoknapatawpha magic would rub off on them. Larry Brown, Willie Morris, Barry Hannah, and the king of the legal thrillers, John Grisham, have all called Oxford home.

Today, Rowan Oak, the sanctuary where Faulkner wrote his greatest works, is owned by the University of Mississippi, which operates the property as a museum. Rowan Oak remains much as Faulkner left it, with his riding boots by the door, his black manual typewriter on display in the study, and the outline of his Pulitzer Prize–winning novel, *A Fable,* scribbled in his handwriting on the wall.

The library on the campus of the University of Mississippi—where Faulkner was briefly such a lackluster student—displays first-edition prints of his novels and early handwritten manuscripts. The inscription on the library's wall was excerpted from the optimistic conclusion of Faulkner's Nobel Prize acceptance speech: "I decline to accept the end of man. I believe that man will not merely endure, he will prevail."

THE NATCHEZ PILGRIMAGE

1931

The city of Natchez is best known as a bastion of the antebellum South. Prior to the Civil War, more than half the millionaires in America lived in this small city on the Mississippi River, erecting palatial mansions with fortunes built on cotton. Natchez surrendered to Union forces early in the conflict, and as a result, the city was spared the burning and destruction suffered by much of the South. All told, Natchez boasts an incredible five hundred surviving antebellum structures, including white-columned mansions, stately town homes, and ornate churches.

Following the Civil War, the devastated economy of the South made it impossible for the city to regain its pre-War economic status. While the war bankrupted many of the owners of the grand mansions, the banks that held the mortgages on the property did not foreclose—after all, what did they want with mansions they could not sell? The owners of the majestic mansions closed off rooms they could not afford to heat and maintained the old homes as best they could.

But even when the South began its slow recovery, Natchez continued to struggle. A gradual loss of river traffic left the city isolated.

Natchez was well on its way to becoming a forgotten city when a late freeze, a bold group of women, and the public's appreciation for the romance of the Old South came together to create a one-of-a-kind event. The grand southern tradition of the pilgrimage—an annual event held in cities throughout Mississippi and marked by tours of antebellum homes—was born in Natchez in 1931.

That year, a late freeze murdered all of the town's blooms the weekend before a meeting of the Mississippi Federation of Garden Clubs was to be held in Natchez. The highlight of the meeting was to have been a tour of the gardens, which were now filled with dead flowers. In a daring move the members of the Natchez Garden Club decided to open their antebellum homes for tour instead. Many of the ladies were hesitant to participate. Times had been hard in Natchez in the six decades since the Civil War, they argued. Their homes had never been remodeled to keep up with the times; many of them were still exactly as they had been before the war.

In the end the very fact that the homes had *not* been remodeled and had retained their antebellum architecture, decor, and personalities ultimately made the tour a success. Visitors were impressed not only with the mansions themselves, but by the fact that they had been continuously lived in for over a century. Unlike historic structures operated as lifeless museums, the houses of Natchez were still *real* homes, many occupied by descendents of the original owners.

As Roane Fleming Byrnes of the Natchez Garden Club wrote, "This substitution aroused such enthusiasm among the visitors that certain members of the Garden Club realized that Natchez's historic mansions were a rare possession which the outside world should share."

The following spring the ladies staged the first official Natchez Pilgrimage Week, charging a modest admission fee and marketing the event under the slogan, "Step into the past with Natchez, where the Old South still lives." By 1933 the event had grown into a well-organized, commercial endeavor, with the seventy-two members of the garden club organized into committees to handle "literature and advertising, poster, program, ball, tour, transportation, and registration."

The early pilgrimages rose to a level of pageantry not seen in Natchez since before the Civil War. While bringing the Old South to life also meant touching upon some disturbing elements of that era, including the practice of slavery, both the white and black citizens of Natchez participated in Pilgrimage Week. In describing the 1933 event Byrnes wrote:

> *The club advertised and opened to the public twenty-four antebellum houses, furnished and intact, some them built as early as the 1780s. The 'pilgrims' were conducted over moss-hung roadways once Indian trails to white-columned mansions where they were received as honored guests by ladies in hoopskirts. . . . In the shops, interesting relics were displayed and at night historic tableaux and old-fashioned balls helped further to reconstruct life in the deep South of a hundred years ago. The Negro citizens of Natchez, sponsored by the Garden Club, made a valuable contribution by singing spirituals, devoting the proceeds of their entertainment to improving their Colonial church.*

By 1934 Pilgrimage Week was bringing some 5,000 visitors to Natchez, a town of just 13,000 residents. By 1935 the event had become the primary fundraiser for the Natchez Garden Club. Profits from the pilgrimage allowed the club to sponsor many beautification and historic preservation projects in the town, and eventually, to purchase and renovate other historic homes and properties in Natchez and open them for tours.

The ladies of the Natchez Garden Club had come upon an idea that would not only promote the history and culture of their town, but that over the coming decades, would also bring hundreds of thousands of tourists—and their money—to Natchez. Byrnes wrote:

> Natchez [had] found herself side-tracked from the main highways of travel . . . she began to lose progress and was gradually becoming 'the forgotten town.' Her citizens, accustomed to the architectural and historic treasures of their community, did not fully appreciate their unique value. . . . The Pilgrimage brought to Natchez thousands of enthusiastic guests from every state in the Union – writers, artists, editors, architects, educators, [and] groups of students. Natchez suddenly awoke from threatened oblivion to find herself famous, praised in magazines and papers all over the country. . . . The dreamy old town felt the thrill of renewed life.

Seeing the success of the Natchez Pilgrimage, other towns in Mississippi, including Columbus, Holly Springs, and Vicksburg, began their own annual pilgrimage events. While each town put its own stamp on the event, all featured tours of antebellum homes as their focal point.

With the exception of 1943–1945, when the event was suspended due to World War II, springtime in Natchez has been synonymous with the pilgrimage. Today, more than eight decades since that first impromptu tour, the event is not only the highlight of the year but is also one of the biggest businesses in Natchez. While most Mississippi pilgrimages last for a week or a weekend, the Natchez extravaganza goes on for a full month in the spring, with another pilgrimage tour offered in the fall. No experience on earth is as thoroughly southern. Costumed hostesses recite each home's history, from architectural details to ghost stories to the family recipe for mint juleps. Visitors marvel at antique Aubusson carpets, hand-blocked Zuber wallpaper, marble fireplace mantels hand-carved in Italy, and fine furniture shipped from France more than two centuries ago. Horse-and-carriage rigs clip-clop through downtown, and colorful displays put on by generations-old camellias, magnolias, and azaleas remind visitors that this spring spectacular began as a garden tour.

While Pilgrimage Week remains a highlight, tours of Natchez's antebellum homes are no longer limited to the event. Around a dozen of the spectacular mansions are now open for tours year-round, with some forty homes doubling as upscale bed-and-breakfast inns.

When the ladies of the Natchez Garden Club cautiously opened their doors in 1931, they could never have imagined that their old family homes would become an attraction that would entice generations of visitors and help bring prosperity to their city.

THE KING IS BORN

1935

On January 8, 1935, a poor couple in Tupelo welcomed a baby boy, born in the humble, two-room house where the struggling couple lived. The baby was a twin, but sadly, his older brother, Jessie, was stillborn. The couple, Vernon and Gladys Presley, named their surviving baby Elvis.

From those humble beginnings, Elvis Presley would go on to influence the world with his talent and charisma, building an entertainment empire and a fortune his careworn parents could never have imagined and becoming recognized worldwide as the King of Rock 'n' Roll.

Vernon Presley borrowed $180 to construct the shotgun house where the future king was born. Two years after Elvis's birth, the Presleys were evicted when Vernon was sent to jail for altering a check and Gladys couldn't repay the modest loan. Elvis and his mother lived with relatives while Elvis's father served an eight-month prison sentence. The small family continued to struggle financially through Elvis's elementary school years at East Tupelo Consolidated School.

A high point came when Elvis was ten years old; his vocal rendition of "Old Shep" won him fifth place in a local talent show. A few months later, Gladys bought her son his first guitar from the Tupelo Hardware Store. She actually took Elvis there to pick out a bicycle, but when a rifle caught his eye, mother and son compromised on the guitar.

In 1948 Elvis and his parents moved to Memphis, Tennessee, where they lived in a housing project for low-income families. Elvis, a shy boy from the wrong side of the tracks, enrolled in Humes High School. Ironically, the future King of Rock and Roll was not popular among his peers, most of whom regarded him as a strange loner who played "hillbilly music" on his guitar during the lunch period.

Elvis never formally studied music. He was influenced by the pop and country music of the day, and also by the gospel music he heard in the Assembly of God church he attended faithfully and the blues music he heard while hanging out on Memphis's Beale Street. In 1953, the same year he graduated from high school, Elvis walked into Sun Records in Memphis and asked to record a demo record as a present for his mother. Intrigued by what he heard, Sun producer Sam Phillips brought Elvis back into the studio for a session with two Sun musicians. Elvis's rendition of a song titled "That's All Right," was the magic bullet Phillips had been listening for, a performance "by a white man that had the Negro sound and the Negro feel." From there, Elvis began recording and touring, appearing in live venues and on television programs.

In 1955 Elvis signed on with manager Colonel Tom Parker, who struck a deal with RCA Victor to acquire Elvis's Sun Records contract for an unprecedented $40,000. At twenty years old, Elvis was still legally a minor, so his father, Vernon, had to sign the contract on his behalf. Elvis's first RCA single, "Heartbreak Hotel," was a number one hit. His first album, titled simply *Elvis Presley,* was the first rock 'n' roll album in history to top the *Billboard* chart. In 1956 Elvis made his movie debut in the film *Love Me Tender*. Elvis Presley, the poor boy born in a shotgun shack in Tupelo, had become an international superstar.

With a sound and a performance style that combined diverse musical influences and challenged social and racial barriers, Elvis Presley ushered in a new era not only in American music, but also in American popular culture. The King of Rock 'n' Roll would go on to record 150 albums and singles that have been certified gold, platinum, or multi-platinum by the Recording Industry Association of America; star in thirty-three movies; appear on numerous television shows, including his own specials; sell out concert venues and Las Vegas shows; and win three Grammy Awards. Globally, Elvis has sold more than one billion record units, more than any other artist in recording history.

The King of Rock 'n' Roll died in 1977 at the age of forty-two. More than 80,000 mourners from around the world lined the streets as the funeral procession made its way from Graceland, Elvis's mansion and final residence in Memphis, to the city's Forest Hill Cemetery. Following an attempt to steal his body, Elvis's remains were reinterred in the grounds of Graceland. In 1982 the mansion was opened for public tours. Graceland attracts more than 500,000 visitors each year and is the second-most toured house in America, topped only by the White House.

Much less grand but far more touching is Elvis's first home, that tiny shotgun house in Tupelo. When Elvis hit the big time, he returned to Tupelo and performed a benefit concert to raise money to build a park for disadvantaged children. The property purchased for the park included Elvis's first home, which is now a popular attraction for diehard Elvis fans and curious tourists. The birthplace's faded, flowered linoleum and worn furnishings are a sharp contrast to the sequined jumpsuits and extravagant lifestyle usually associated with the King of Rock 'n' Roll. The entire structure is just 450 square feet; Graceland holds a sofa longer than the entire house. A museum behind the house features clothing, photographs, records, and other Elvis memorabilia donated by a family friend.

The most poignant display in the museum is a quotation from the King himself. Stenciled on the wall are Elvis's own words: "I could never become so rich that I would forget what it's like to be poor."

THE MURDER OF EMMETT TILL

1955

He was just a fourteen-year-old boy horsing around, a visiting teenager from Chicago trying to impress his Mississippi relatives by whistling at a pretty older woman. But the boy was black, the woman was white, and the place was Mississippi in 1955. That harmless wolf whistle cost the boy, Emmett Till, his life.

According to family members, Till was a "fun-loving, gentle person who loved practical jokes and making other people laugh." In the summer of 1955, Till traveled from Chicago, where he lived with his mother, Mamie Till-Bradley, to the Mississippi Delta for a visit with his great-uncle, Mose Wright and his cousins. At the time Till visited, Jim Crow laws were in effect in Mississippi to enforce segregation between blacks and whites, and societal standards of black and white behavior were even stricter than the letter of the law. A native of Mississippi who had moved to Chicago as a child, Till's mother was aware of the need to prepare her son for his Mississippi visit.

"I began lecturing and schooling [Emmett] seriously on how to conduct himself in the South," Mamie Till-Bradley wrote in a 1956 memoir. "I emphasized over and over again to him that it was not the same as . . . Chicago and he had to be extra careful to avoid getting in trouble with white people. . . . I told him that if anything happened, even though you think you're perfectly within your right, for goodness' sake take low. If necessary, get on your knees and beg apologies. Don't cross anybody down there because Mississippi is not like Chicago. What you can get away with here, you might not be able to do it there. I said no matter how much it seems that you have the right, just forget your rights while you're in Mississippi."

On August 24, 1955, Till and his cousins visited Bryant's Grocery and Meat Market, a country store that sold food and sundries to black sharecroppers in the dusty little community of Money. Till purchased a package of bubble gum from Carolyn Bryant, the twenty-one-year-old wife of the store's owner. The exact details of what followed between the white woman and the visiting black boy have never been confirmed. Bryant would later testify that Till grabbed her wrist and waist, asked her, "How about a date, baby?" and made obscene, sexually suggestive comments to her. Other witnesses stated that nothing at all was said inside the store, that Till simply paid Bryant for his bubble gum and left. What all the witnesses agreed upon was that when Bryant exited the store shortly after Till stepped outside, the boy whistled at her, apparently acting on a dare made by other black teenagers gathered on the store's front porch.

Days later on August 28, Carolyn's husband, Roy Bryant, and his half-brother, J. W. Milam, arrived at Mose Wright's home at 2:30 a.m., accompanied by at least one other person and armed with a flashlight and a pistol, and demanded to see, "the boy that done the talking down at Money." Wright showed them to the bedroom where Emmett Till and his own son, Simeon, were sharing a bed. Bryant and Milam ordered Till to get dressed. Wright's wife pleaded with the men not to take Till, offering to pay the men "for whatever he might have done." Bryant and Milam ignored her pleas and marched Till to the door, telling Wright they planned only to "take him up the road and whip him," and then bring him back to the house. As they left, Milam asked Mose Wright how old he was. When Wright replied, "sixty-four," Milam said, "Well, if you know any of us here tonight, you will never live to get to be sixty-five."

Bryant and Milam drove fourteen-year-old Till to a nearby barn, where they tortured and beat him for hours, crushing his skull, breaking his wrist and leg, and partially gouging out his eye. The men then shot the wounded boy in the head, lashed a seventy-five-pound cotton gin fan to his neck with barbed wire, and dumped his mangled remains into the Tallahatchie River. Three days later, a fisherman spotted Till's battered body floating in the muddy water.

Till's remains were returned to his mother in Chicago, where Mamie Till-Bradley stunned the nation by holding a public funeral service with an open casket, displaying the mutilated body of her son as a graphic example of the horrors happening to black Americans in the South and declaring, "I wanted the world to see what they did to my baby." More than 50,000 people attended Till's funeral, and hundreds of thousands more saw the images of his disfigured body published in magazines and newspapers nationwide.

With America's attention focused on the murder and on the issue of civil rights in Mississippi, Bryant and Milam were indicted for the murder of Emmett Till. Held in Tallahatchie County, the five-day, standing-room-only murder trial attracted national publicity. Bryant and Milam confessed to kidnapping Till, but claimed they had let him go and that he had simply disappeared. The prosecution questioned Mamie Till-Bradley's identification of the body pulled from the river, producing "expert" witnesses who claimed that the body appeared to have been in the river longer than the time Till had been missing, and suggesting that decomposition had made the remains impossible to positively identify as those of Till. With no positive identification, the prosecutor argued, there was no proof Till had been murdered at all; perhaps he was still alive and hiding in Chicago.

Mamie Till-Bradley attended the trial, listening to five days of testimony, including that of witnesses who spoke to the upstanding character of the men who had murdered her child. When the jury left the courtroom to deliberate, Till-Bradley left the courthouse, telling her family members there was no point in staying; the verdict would be "not guilty."

She was right. Despite the brave testimony of Mose Wright to the kidnapping, the testimony of witnesses who heard screaming and the sounds of a beating coming from the barn and saw Bryant and Milam exiting the barn, and still more testimony from witnesses who saw blood dripping from a covered tarp in the bed of Milam's pickup truck, the all-white jury acquitted Bryant and Milam. Every member of the jury later acknowledged being contacted by representatives of the Citizen's Council, an organization founded to preserve seg-regation in the South, to ensure they would vote "the right way." A grand jury met in November of 1955 to consider kidnapping charges against Bryant and Milam but failed to indict them.

With double jeopardy attached and no possibility they could be retried, Bryant and Milam confessed to the murder in an inter-view with *Look* magazine. Published in January of 1956, the article by reporter William Bradford Huie titled "The Shocking Story of Approved Killing in Mississippi," came with a $3,000 payment to Bryant and Milam and a $1,000 payment to their lawyer.

Letters to the editor of *Look* in response to the article reflected the turmoil of the era and the polarized opinions on the civil rights issue. Reactions ranged from, "Minorities all over the country are indebted to your stand on this brutal slaying," to "Roy Bryant and J.W. Milam did what had to be done, and their courage in taking the course they did is to be commended," to "If this case is not reopened and the guilty punished, I shall laugh at the word 'justice.'"

The overwhelming reaction, however, was outrage. The sheer brutality of the crime, combined with the fact that the victim was a fourteen-year-old child, shocked and horrified even staunch support-ers of segregation. Editorials and letters to Mississippi newspapers expressed shame and revulsion. One editorial proclaimed, "Now is the time for every citizen who loves the state of Mississippi to stand up and be counted before hoodlum white trash brings us to destruction."

Bryant and Milam became pariahs in their home state. The Bry-ant Grocery went bankrupt, neither man could find a bank willing to loan them money for farming, and they were forced to leave Mis-sissippi to seek work in Texas. Roy and Carolyn Bryant divorced. Both men eventually returned to Mississippi, where Bryant opened a small store in the Delta and later served time in prison for food stamp fraud. By 1994 both men had died.

The murder of Emmett Till was credited with raising national awareness of the deplorable treatment of blacks in the South, and inspiring later heroes of the civil rights movement, including Rosa Parks, to take a stand for what was just. Till's murder was the catalyst for the Civil Rights Act of 1957, which allowed the US Department of Justice to intervene in local cases when civil rights were being compromised.

In 2004 one year after Mamie Till-Bradley's death, the Emmett Till case was reopened. It had long been suspected that Bryant and Milam had not acted alone; the US Department of Justice launched a new investigation to determine if anyone else had been involved and could yet be prosecuted for the murder. As part of the investigation, Till's body was exhumed and the remains were positively identified as those of Emmett Till. Till was reinterred in a new casket, and the original casket was donated to the Smithsonian Institution.

The investigation did not result in any additional prosecutions. Simeon Wright, Emmett Till's cousin who had been sleeping in the bed with him the night he was kidnapped and murdered, expressed frustration, saying, "Every last person up until now has gotten away with murder. It looks like for justice in this world, they have gotten away with it. But eventually, in the end, I think they're all going to pay for it."

Following Mamie Till-Bradley's death, a family member said that what Emmett Till's mother had wanted more than anything else was an apology. It didn't happen in her lifetime, but in 2007 officials in Tallahatchie County issued an official apology to the Till family for the terrible crime against Emmett Till and for failing to bring his murderers to justice and unveiled a marker commemorating Till's death.

"Back in 1955, Tallahatchie County did nothing to help us," Simeon Wright said on behalf of the family. "This is all they can do, and we appreciate it and accept it."

Today in Glendora just a few miles from the dilapidated remains of the Bryant Grocery and Meat Market, the Emmett Till Historic Intrepid Center pays tribute to the boy who lost his life, but whose death inspired others to fight for equality.

IT TAKES A
ROCKET SCIENTIST

1961

In the late 1960s and early 1970s, a common saying in southwest Mississippi was, "If you want to go to the moon, you have to go through Hancock County, Mississippi, to get there."

In 1961 the National Aeronautics and Space Administration (NASA) announced the purchase of 13,500 acres of remote woodland and swampland in southwest Mississippi for the construction of Mississippi Test Operations, a massive facility designed for the test firing of Saturn and Nova booster rockets, the powerful rockets that would propel mankind into space. This previously quiet, unspoiled tract of land had become a critical stop on the way to the moon.

"I was overwhelmed by the beauty of the scenery on the Mississippi site," Dr. Werner von Braun, director of NASA's Marshal Space Flight Center, said in 1963, as construction was underway. "I felt a little sorry over the fact that bulldozers will soon be going into the area and tearing up some of that beauty. But if NASA didn't come to [Mississippi], we'd never get to the moon."

At the time NASA announced the location of the facility, the agency was spending $14 million a day on ventures related to space exploration. A significant portion of those funds were spent in the southern United States, with massive projects launched in Texas, Louisiana, Mississippi, Alabama, and Florida, five states that came to be known as the "Southern Crescent" and the "Space Frontier." Those historically rural states saw a sudden influx of thousands of federal employees, battalions of construction workers, hundreds of new government facilities, and thousands of new jobs. Along with rockets and engines came new schools and service businesses, a soaring housing market and property values, new roads and sewers, never-before-experienced traffic jams, and next-door neighbors who were real-life rocket scientists.

The Mississippi site was chosen both because it offered large tracts of undeveloped land and for its proximity to NASA operations in New Orleans, Louisiana, and Huntsville, Alabama. The engines tested in Mississippi would be manufactured at NASA's Michoud plant in New Orleans about thirty-five miles away and then transported by barge to the Mississippi Test Operation facility. After testing, the engines would be barged across the Gulf of Mexico for firing at Cape Canaveral, Florida.

In Mississippi NASA purchased not only 13,500 acres in Hancock and Pearl River Counties for the construction of the test facility itself, but also easement rights to another 128,000 acres surrounding the site to serve as a buffer zone against noise and the possible danger of explosion. The $750 million project was the largest construction project in the history of the state of Mississippi and the second largest in the United States at that time, bringing 6,000 construction workers to the once-remote Mississippi swampland.

But not everyone was thrilled to see NASA come to Mississippi. Some 660 families living on the land purchased for the site and buffer zone were forced to relocate, sacrificing homes and property that had been in their families for generations. After 174 years in existence, the entire town of Gainesville, Mississippi, ceased to exist, forced into extinction by the location of the NASA facility. Around 500 Gainesville residents relocated, two cemeteries were moved, and an old swimming hole used for hundreds of baptisms became a part of the waterway serving the NASA test site. By the time the first rocket was test fired, Gainesville was only a memory.

Upon completion, the facility initially employed more than 2,600 permanent workers, including engineers, scientists, technicians, and support personnel, all of them dedicated to propelling the first man to the moon. The focal points of the development were towering test stands in which the rockets were "static fired," or fired while held in place on the stands rather than actually launched into space. While it would have been possible to launch the rockets from the Mississippi site, a malfunction could have resulted in debris falling over populated areas. Each static test stand stood as tall as a thirty-story building; each of their foundations held more than 1,600 cubic yards of concrete and 1,020 tons of reinforcing steel. Each stand was capable of holding a blazing engine in place for two minutes. During the test firing, the pad beneath the test stand was, for those 120 seconds, the hottest spot on the globe.

Mississippi Test Operations' original mission was to flight certify all stages of the Saturn V rocket for the Apollo program. The first test firing in Mississippi took place on April 23, 1966. Less than nine years after NASA broke ground in Mississippi, astronauts Neil Armstrong and Buzz Aldrin walked on the moon, safely transported there by a space vehicle whose boosters were tested and proven flight-worthy in Mississippi.

Over the next five decades, every stage of every vehicle involving a manned mission would be test fired in Mississippi. When the Apollo program ended in the early 1970s, the Mississippi facility, by then known as the National Space Technology Laboratories, assumed responsibility for test firing all of the space shuttle main engines. The facility tested engines used in 135 shuttle missions over a thirty-four-year span. In that time not a single mission failed due to engine malfunction.

In 1988, President Ronald Reagan renamed the facility the John C. Stennis Space Center (SSC) in honor of Mississippian and US Senator John C. Stennis in recognition of his leadership and support of the nation's space program. SSC conducted the last test of a space shuttle main engine in July of 2009. By 2012, Stennis Space Center was testing NASA's J-2X powerpack component and engine, a system capable of transporting man deeper into space than ever before. SSC also partners with private sector companies to test the engines that will someday enable commercial space flights.

Over the five decades after its founding, the Stennis Space Center has evolved into a multidisciplinary research and development facility that houses not only NASA, but also thirty other agencies and companies working in environmental science programs and national defense. Resident agencies include the Naval Meteorology and Oceanography Command, the largest concentration of oceanographers in the world, as well as the Naval Research Laboratory, the Navy's corporate laboratory.

NASA's Speakers Bureau at Stennis sends scientists and engineers for lectures and presentations to civic groups and schools throughout the South. The 72,000-square-foot Infinity Center at Stennis features hands-on educational exhibits and activities related to space exploration and work conducted at Stennis and offers guided tours of the Stennis Space Center.

Today, more than 5,300 scientists, engineers, business people, and support personnel report to work at Mississippi's John C. Stennis Space Center. History was originally made on this land in the 1700s, when the first white settlers carved a new life out of its unexplored wilderness. Today, history is still being made here by a new generation of men and women committed to unlocking the vast frontiers of the universe.

JAMES MEREDITH
INTEGRATES OLE MISS

1962

The University of Mississippi in Oxford, affectionately referred to as "Ole Miss," is known for its lovely, tree-shaded campus, its Rebel athletic teams, and its nationally renowned Honors College. But in 1962, Ole Miss made international news as the scene of deadly riots sparked by the enrollment of James Meredith, the first black student in the university's 114-year history.

The civil rights movement was underway in the American South when Meredith, a twenty-nine-year-old, married, former serviceman in the US Air Force and a student at all-black Jackson State College (now Jackson State University), applied for admission to Ole Miss, the state's flagship university.

In his memoir, *A Mission from God: A Memoir and a Challenge for America*, Meredith wrote:

> *I was fifteen when I first fully appreciated the personal impact of white supremacy. My brother and I were*

*riding the train home from Chicago on the famous
train called The City of New Orleans. At Memphis,
we were ordered to vacate our seats and move to the
'colored car' as we were about to enter Mississippi. It
was overcrowded and we had to stand. Tears rolled
down my cheeks for the rest of the trip, and in that
moment, I swore to myself that I would devote my life
to changing the degraded position of black people in
the world.*

*[Years later], I chose as my target the University
of Mississippi, which in 1960 was the holiest temple
of white supremacy in America. . . . I reasoned that
if I could enter the University of Mississippi as its
first known black student, I would fracture the system
of state-enforced white supremacy in Mississippi. It
would drive a stake into the heart of the beast. If I
managed to not get killed or chased off, I could create
an earth-shaking precedent in Mississippi.*

Meredith received a routine "welcome" letter from Ole Miss
when he initially applied, but his application was denied when the
university's registrar learned he was black. Meredith filed a lawsuit
against the university, alleging racial discrimination. The case was
eventually settled on appeal by the US Supreme Court, which ruled
in Meredith's favor in September 1962.

State officials attempted to defy the Supreme Court decision
with various legal appeals that resulted in a constitutional conflict
between the State of Mississippi and the US government. Leading
that effort was Mississippi Governor Ross Barnett, who on September 20, 1962, personally blocked the entrance to the university
offices and denied Meredith admission. Barnett evoked laughter

from those present when he asked Meredith and the all-white group of US marshals assigned to protect him, "Which one of you is James Meredith?"

"I almost laughed myself," Meredith wrote in his memoir. "It was a funny line. The federal officials . . . seemed stunned. They didn't understand the Mississippi game, but Barnett and I sure did."

Again accompanied by a contingent of federal marshals, Meredith tried to enroll three more times and each time was denied, twice by Barnett and once by Lieutenant Governor Paul Johnson.

On the night of Saturday, September 29, Governor Barnett addressed 46,000 wildly cheering, Confederate flag–waving fans at an Ole Miss football game played in the state capital of Jackson. His fifteen-word address—"I love Mississippi. I love her people. Our customs. I love and respect our heritage."—whipped the already on-edge crowd into a frenzy. What no one in the crowd knew at the time was that Barnett had already seen the writing on the wall. He realized that despite various motions and appeals still moving through the court system, Meredith would eventually be enrolled under order of the US Supreme Court. Even as Barnett postured for the crowds and cameras, he was in discussions with President John Kennedy and Attorney General Robert Kennedy about how to enroll Meredith without losing political face or inciting a violent clash.

But the time for a peaceful enrollment of Meredith had passed. On Sunday, September 30, some four hundred armed federal marshals acting under the direction of Attorney General Kennedy arrived on the Ole Miss campus. James Meredith was quietly brought on campus and taken to his assigned dormitory. The plan was to secretly enroll him that night, and then announce on Monday that the battle was over.

The plan failed. As crowds gathered, the marshals formed a ring around the Lyceum, the antebellum administration building that was the geographic and symbolic heart of the Ole Miss campus. Members of the Mississippi Highway Patrol took positions between the marshals and a growing crowd of students, spectators, reporters, and segregationists, including many who came from outside Mississippi. Inside the Lyceum, officials from the US Justice Department and the University of Mississippi waited for a scheduled national address from President John Kennedy, who planned to announce that federal forces were on campus to ensure that Meredith was enrolled without incident.

As the marshals held their position into the evening, the crowd began to taunt them, then to pelt them with cigarette butts and gravel, then with rocks, bottles, and bricks. When a lead pipe knocked a marshal to the ground, James McShane, the chief federal marshal, gave the order to fire tear gas into the crowd. The scene exploded into a violent, chaotic riot.

Members of the Mississippi Highway Patrol attempted to block access to the university, but with the campus open and wooded on all sides, hundreds of enraged segregationists, many of them armed, entered the campus and joined in the riot. Twenty thousand federal troops were ordered into action and reported to the Ole Miss campus to help restore order; President Kennedy also federalized the Mississippi National Guard. The pastoral Ole Miss campus had become a war zone. The heavy use of the tear gas made areas of the campus unapproachable, cars burned in the streets, glass and debris littered the sidewalks, and gunshots and screams filled the air. Two people, a French journalist named Paul Guihard and a twenty-year-old bystander named Ray Gunter, were shot and killed during the melee. Their assailants were never identified. More than two hundred more people were seriously injured.

Weeks later, Ole Miss chancellor John D. Williams said,

In that night of horrors, I wondered whether any other chancellor had ever had cause to feel such anguish. . . . The University had become a pawn in a combat between powerful political forces. With little consultation with administrative officers . . . the effective control of the university was taken out of our hands. The Lyceum—which even during the Civil War had been a hospital, a place of mercy—had become a battle post.

The riot lasted for some fourteen hours. By mid-morning, federal troops had restored some sense of order. It had been waged at tremendous cost, but the battle was over. On October 1, 1962, James Meredith enrolled as the first black student in the history of the University of Mississippi. Meredith attended two classes that day; his third class was cancelled because the building in which it was held was still filled with tear gas.

Asked by reporters if he felt any guilt over the riots, Meredith responded, "I'm very sorry that anyone had to get hurt or killed. Of course, that's an unfair question of me. I don't believe any of you think I had anything to do with that."

For months following the riots, federal marshals accompanied Meredith as he attended class; Meredith wrote that he "was more heavily guarded than the President of the United States." But while he was never welcomed and was constantly verbally harassed, Meredith's presence triggered no more mob violence on the Ole Miss campus. Meredith graduated from the University of Mississippi with a degree in political science in 1963.

Ole Miss and the state of Mississippi were criticized worldwide in the wake of the riots. In remarks delivered on October 31, 1962,

Chancellor Williams said, "Riots, lawlessness, destruction, murder—that is the image of the university and of Mississippi that has been given the whole wide world."

Several years would pass before people outside of Mississippi associated the name, "Ole Miss" with anything other than the violent riot. But gradually, over many years, Ole Miss earned a new reputation as a university committed to racial reconciliation. Forty years following Meredith's arrival on campus and the riots seen around the nation, the University of Mississippi launched a fundraising campaign to erect a permanent memorial on campus honoring James Meredith and other heroes of the civil rights movement in Mississippi. The resulting $150,000 sculpture was funded through donations from students, businesses, private citizens, and state and federal arts grants. The completed memorial stands between the historic Lyceum and the John D. Williams Library near the center of the Ole Miss campus.

In 2008 the university was once again thrust into the national spotlight when Ole Miss, the university that once responded to integration with race riots, hosted a presidential debate between John McCain and Barack Obama, the first African-American candidate for president of the United States.

"For many people, 1962 is locked in their memory, as far as Ole Miss is concerned," said then-chancellor Robert Khayat. "Now, forty-six years later, we're hosting the presidential debates and one of the candidates is an African American. I think that speaks volumes about where we were and where we are."

James Meredith, the man who sparked such controversy in 1962, is today an enigmatic figure. In 2012 the University of Mississippi marked the fiftieth anniversary of Meredith's enrollment with ceremonies and seminars examining the university's historic integration and its subsequent progress in race relations. Meredith declined to attend.

But while his relationship with his alma mater is a complicated and painful one, Meredith frequently wears an Ole Miss baseball cap in public. He attended a 2012 Ole Miss football game in Oxford as a guest in the chancellor's skybox, and when his presence was announced over the loudspeaker, the home crowd stood and cheered. University of Mississippi Chancellor Dan Jones recognized Meredith's contributions in a letter written to Meredith fifty years after he integrated the Ole Miss campus:

> *Your determination to enroll under the most difficult conditions and to successfully complete your degree in the midst of constant hostility was a turning point in the life of our university, station, and nation. It was instrumental in changing lives not just for black Americans, but for all of us.*

THE WORLD'S FIRST LUNG AND HEART TRANSPLANTS

1963 and 1964

They not only said that it *couldn't* be done, they said it *shouldn't* be done.

In 1963 the idea of transplanting organs from one human being to another was still the stuff of science fiction and a moral gray area. But Dr. James Hardy, professor of surgery and chairman of the surgical department at the University of Mississippi Medical Center (UMMC), believed not only that it *could* be done, but that it *should* be done.

Dr. Hardy realized that perfecting organ transplants could ultimately save hundreds of thousands of lives. For years he conducted research geared toward making the transplantation of major human organs possible. In June of 1963 headlines around the world told the astounding news of a surgical team in Jackson, Mississippi, that had transplanted a human donor's lung into another human's body for the first time in history. The patient, a seriously ill inmate incarcerated at the Mississippi penitentiary, died eighteen days later of renal failure unrelated to the transplant, but Dr. Hardy had proven that a human lung transplant was possible.

"The management of public interest posed a problem almost equal to that of transplantation of the lung itself," Dr. Hardy wrote in his memoir, *The World of Surgery, 1945–1985: Memoirs of One Participant.* "The degree of acceptance of the operation varied with almost every individual. Some considered the transplantation unethical or even immoral. . . . Of course, when a startling new treatment proves successful, its ethical problems are immediately abolished. Had our lung transplant patient lived a year or more, in comfortable health, criticism relevant to unethical procedure would have been muted."

On January 23, 1964, Dr. Hardy again made headlines with another organ transplant. But this time, the headlines were even more controversial. Dr. Hardy's team had transplanted the heart of a chimpanzee—man's closest relative—into the chest of a human patient. The patient, Boyd Rush, was dying; the transplant was a last-ditch, groundbreaking effort to save his life. As Dr. Hardy later wrote, "we would not have risked the life of a patient who might otherwise have lived days longer."

The chimpanzee heart beat for ninety minutes inside Rush's chest before stopping.

The surgery "precipitated intense ethical, moral, social, religious, financial, governmental, and even legal concerns," Dr. Hardy wrote. "We had not transplanted merely a human heart, we had transplanted a *subhuman* heart."

Following the transplant, Hardy and the University of Mississippi Medical Center were bombarded with harsh criticism.

"Public media reporters from around the world seemed to come out of the woodwork," Dr. Hardy wrote. "We had never been exposed to such massive public interest."

Many members of the press and the general public were horrified by the radical experiment. Their complaints were voiced from the long-held perspective that the heart was the dwelling place of the human soul. To dare to replace such a vital organ with that of a monkey was, they argued, nothing short of blasphemy.

"At that time, the heart still carried strong emotional overtones," Dr. Hardy wrote. "'I love you with all my heart and soul,' or 'heartfelt,' or 'no heart for it,' or 'heartsick,' or 'fainthearted.' How would one lover feel, for instance, if within the other's breast beat the heart of a stranger?"

Some of Hardy's medical colleagues were also critical, arguing that Hardy's work with lab animals was not adequate preparation for such a bold move in human surgery. Fellow surgeon Dr. Thomas Starzl, who had successfully transplanted human kidneys and livers, told Dr. Hardy, "You and I are absolute pariahs in American surgery."

"Although I was considerably depressed and had certainly learned who my friends were (they were far fewer than I'd thought), I still felt we had achieved an important milestone under acceptable ethical and moral circumstances," Dr. Hardy wrote. "When I traveled in Europe, I found that our heart transplant was known everywhere, and instead of all the carping and criticism going on in the United States, many surgical scientists in Europe simply wanted to know why we had not gone right ahead with another one."

Hardy's controversial transplant paved the way for other surgeons, including Dr. Christiaan Barnard, a South African doctor who performed the world's first successful human-donor-to-human-recipient heart transplant in 1967. Dr. Mario Barnard, Christiaan Barnard's brother, assisted in the heart transplant and published a paper in a South African medical journal in which he credited Hardy's Mississippi team with proving that "the feasibility of cardiac transplantation was now irrefutable."

Following the South African transplant, Hardy wrote, "It was obvious that opinion in the United States had changed overnight. . . . Once again I was besieged by reporters, [but] this time there was none of the adversarial hostility that had characterized such interviews in 1964."

Human-to-human heart transplants soon followed at hospitals in the United States. In 1971 the Vishnevsky Institute in Moscow, Russia, honored Dr. Hardy for his pioneering role in transplantation and presented him with two medals—one for the lung transplant and the other for the heart transplant that had been so controversial only a few years earlier.

Over the years Dr. Hardy continued to build his reputation as a medical pioneer and leader. In addition to the first lung and heart transplants, Dr. Hardy's team also performed the first successful human kidney autotransplant and the first human adrenal autotransplant in the United States. An autotransplant involves transplanting tissues from one part of the body to another in the same individual.

Dr. Hardy edited and wrote twenty-three books, including two that became the standard surgery textbooks in American medical schools. He served as a visiting professor at more than thirty-five medical schools in the United States and abroad, while continuing to direct the University of Mississippi Medical Center's surgical department.

Hardy published more than five hundred articles in medical journals and served as editor of multiple international surgical publications and as president of six professional surgical associations, including the International Society of Surgery. The 1983 Surgical Forum of the American College of Surgeons was dedicated to Hardy, recognizing him as "an outstanding surgical educator, investigator, clinical surgeon, and international leader."

In addition to his remarkable achievements in the world medical arena, Dr. Hardy helped generations of Mississippians with his work in their state. As the first chairman of the University of Mississippi Medical Center's Department of Surgery, Hardy directed the focus of the surgical department from its first day in 1955 until he retired in 1987. Hardy served patients and trained the next generation of skilled surgeons, all in the same teaching hospital where he performed his groundbreaking transplants. He remained a friend of UMMC until his death in 2003.

Today, the University of Mississippi Medical Center is home to the only organ transplant program in the state. The first lung and heart transplants performed at the UMMC paved the way for every lung and heart transplant that has followed around the world. Dr. James Hardy later described those first controversial transplant surgeries as "[setting] in motion the inexorable process of human imagination and gradual acceptance which has evolved into our current, almost casual, attitude toward transplantation."

THE NESHOBA COUNTY MURDERS

1964

Perhaps the most infamous chapter in Mississippi history unfolded in the steamy summer of 1964, when three civil rights workers, Andrew Goodman, Michael "Mickey" Schwerner, and James Chaney, vanished in rural Neshoba County.

The summer of 1964 was known as "Freedom Summer," a movement coordinated by civil rights organizations operating in Mississippi, including the Congress of Racial Equality (CORE). Freedom Summer organizers rallied college students, many from outside Mississippi, to come to the state to help run voter registration drives for black Mississippians, teach in "Freedom Schools" opened to educate black Mississippians on their civil rights, and handle other duties instrumental to integrating Mississippi.

The movement's leaders made it clear that participating in the effort could be dangerous. Andrew Goodman was in the audience when two leaders of the effort, Robert Moses and James Foreman, addressed an auditorium packed with prospective volunteers at Western College in Oxford, Ohio. The college was the site of an orientation session for five hundred northern college students who had agreed to spend their summer in Mississippi. According to an article in *Ramparts* magazine, Moses and Foreman "welcomed them to the Mississippi Summer Project and then went on to promise them that they might get killed." Foreman went on to say, "I may be killed. You may be killed. If you recognize that—that you may be killed—the question of whether or not you will be put in jail will become very, very minute."

Moses was followed at the podium by R. Jess Brown, a black lawyer from Mississippi, who explained:

> *Now get this in your heads and remember what I am going to say. They—the police, the county sheriff, the state police—they are all waiting for you. . . . They know some of your names and your descriptions even now, even before you get to Mississippi. They know you are coming and they are ready. All I can do is give you some pointers on how to stay alive. . . . If the police stop you and arrest you, don't get out and argue with the cops and say, 'I know my rights.' There ain't no point in standing there trying to teach them some constitutional law at twelve o'clock at night. Go to jail and wait for your lawyer.*

A requirement of all those volunteering for Freedom Summer was that they raise five hundred dollars in bail money and provide a list of their next of kin.

But even those dire warnings could not deter Goodman, Schwerner, or Chaney. A native of New York, Goodman was an enthusiastic volunteer making his first trip to Mississippi in June of 1964. Also from New York, Mickey Schwerner and his wife, Rita, were experienced volunteer leaders in the CORE field office based in Meridian, Mississippi. James Chaney, a veteran black Mississippi activist, worked alongside them to integrate his home state. All three were in their early twenties, young men passionate about their cause and willing to fight for what they believed was just.

On the morning of June 21, 1964—the day after Goodman first set foot in Mississippi—the three men traveled from their base in Meridian to nearby Philadelphia, a town in Neshoba County, to investigate the burning of Mount Zion Methodist Church, which had served as a meeting place for civil rights activists. On their way back to Meridian late that afternoon, Goodman, Schwerner, and Chaney were arrested, ostensibly for speeding. The arresting officer was Neshoba County Deputy Sheriff Cecil Price, a known member of the Ku Klux Klan. Price held the men in the county jail, denying them the right to make a phone call and instructing his staff that if anyone called looking for them, they were to say the men were not there. After night fell, Price released the three, but followed them in his patrol car to the county line, where he ordered them out of their CORE station wagon and back into his vehicle. Price then turned the workers over to waiting fellow members of the Ku Klux Klan.

When the three men were reported missing by their coworkers, the federal government responded by sending the FBI to Mississippi to investigate—a move that almost certainly would never have happened if Goodman and Schwerner had not been white. While local authorities suggested the men had simply left Mississippi, those on the frontlines of the civil rights movement in the state assumed they were dead. Over the next several weeks, the FBI cultivated local informants while helping lead a search of the backwoods of east Mississippi. Gripping wooden clubs to fend off water moccasins, several hundred searchers, including FBI agents and sailors from the US Navy, sloshed through the area's many swamps, rivers, and creeks.

During the search, Navy divers and the FBI discovered the bodies of at least seven other black Mississippians whose disappearances had attracted no attention outside of their local communities. When the CORE station wagon Goodman, Schwerner, and Chaney had been driving was found burned and dumped in a remote area, the case received national media coverage.

Forty-four days after they were last seen alive, a tip from a paid, confidential informant prompted FBI agents to excavate an earthen dam on a farm just outside of Philadelphia. The bodies of Goodman, Schwerner, and Chaney were buried inside. All three had been shot at close range, Goodman and Schwerner once and Chaney three times. Chaney had also been subjected to a bone-shattering beating. Deputy Cecil Price assisted FBI agents in removing the remains from the makeshift grave.

"I am sorry the three fellows is dead," a black Mississippian told a magazine reporter as national media coverage of the murders reached its height. "But five of us that we know about have been killed this year and nobody raised any hell about it. Now two white boys is dead and all the world comes running to look and see. They never would have done this had just us been dead."

The State of Mississippi initially declined to prosecute any of the known Ku Klux Klan members suspected of the murders. In January of 1965, however, the federal government indicted Price and seventeen others with violation of the victims' civil rights. The defendants included Sam Bowers, imperial wizard of the White Knights of the Ku Klux Klan; Lawrence Rainey, sheriff of Neshoba County; Olen Burrage, owner of the property where the bodies were discovered; Edgar Ray Killen, a part-time minister and sawmill operator; and other members of the Klan. The trial was pending when Price announced his candidacy for sheriff of Neshoba County; he lost the election to one of his codefendants. A guilty verdict was returned against seven of the men, including Price and Bowers. None of those convicted served more than six years.

The case was reopened by the State of Mississippi in the mid-2000s, and on June 21, 2005—exactly forty-one years after the murders—eighty-year-old former Klansman Edgar Ray Killen, the suspected mastermind of the murder plot, was found guilty of manslaughter and sentenced to sixty years in prison.

Chaney, Goodman, and Schwerner's murders sparked national outrage and spurred the passage of the Civil Rights Act of 1964 and the Voting Rights Act of 1965. They were not allowed to live to see the results of their work, but Goodman, Schwerner, and Chaney had brought about the change they had so passionately worked toward and believed in.

Today, a Mississippi historical marker stands at the site of the old Neshoba County jail in Philadelphia where the three men were held hours prior to their murder. The Neshoba County Historical Commission sponsored the project and raised the funds for the marker. A second monument honoring James Chaney, Andrew Goodman, and Michael Schwerner graces the grounds of Mt. Zion Church in Neshoba County, near the same place where the three young men gave their lives for a cause they believed in and forever changed the state where they died.

THE INTERNATIONAL
BALLET COMPETITION

1979

The USA International Ballet Competition (IBC) is a two-week, Olympic-style event in which the world's rising ballet stars compete for gold, silver, and bronze medals, cash awards, scholarships, and jobs. The audience is filled with ballet company directors from around the globe searching for the world's greatest dancing talent, ballet enthusiasts moved to tears and ovations by the performances they are privileged to witness, and aspiring dancers hoping to someday find themselves dancing for the gold.

The first International Ballet Competition premiered in Varna, Bulgaria, in 1964 and eventually grew into a series of high-profile competitions that rotated among the cities of Varna and Moscow in Russia, and Tokyo, Japan. When a fourth city in the United States was added to the rotation, the choice of settings for the prestigious event dubbed "the Olympics of Dance" was not New York, Boston, or Chicago, but Jackson, Mississippi.

Mississippi's journey to hosting the competition began in 1975, when the Jackson Ballet Guild invited Thalia Mara, a renowned dancer and instructor, to develop a professional ballet company and school in the state of Mississippi. Born in Chicago to Russian parents, Mara had begun her dance career at an early age and gone on to perform on stages around the world. As an acclaimed instructor, she created the School of Ballet Repertory in New York City, the first school of its kind in the United States to offer elementary and secondary academics as well as the performing arts. When Mara left New York to accept the position in Mississippi, her goals included educating not only dancers, but also audiences. In Mississippi Mara helped build an appreciation for ballet among those who had no previous knowledge of the art.

As a part of her development plan, the ambitious Mara convinced city leaders that it would be possible to secure the USA International Ballet Competition for the city of Jackson. Mara knew of a group of dance enthusiasts in New York City who were searching for a home for the first US International Ballet Competition. With their assistance, Mara helped found the nonprofit corporation Mississippi Ballet International, Inc. to produce the event.

The first USA International Ballet Competition was held in Jackson in June of 1979. The state of Mississippi welcomed seventy dancers from fifteen countries, as well as an esteemed international panel of jurors chaired by the legendary Robert Joffrey, artistic director of the acclaimed Joffrey Ballet, and including the Soviet Union's Yuri Grigorovitch, director of the Bolshoi Ballet. During its inaugural year, the USA IBC became the first international ballet competition to also host an International Dance School, which provided students and competitors with the opportunity to study under renowned dancers and instructors.

When planning began for the first competition, most people in Mississippi were unaware of the importance of the event in the world of dance. But as patrons came to see the dancers perform and spread word of the caliber of their performances, the excitement grew. Tickets to later rounds of the competition and the final awards gala sold out, and Mississippians soon realized the magnitude of the cultural event that had come to their state.

At the conclusion of the first competition, the Jackson event was sanctioned by the International Dance Committee of the International Theater Institute of the United Nations Educational, Scientific, and Cultural Organization (UNESCO), and Jackson, Mississippi, took its place alongside Varna, Moscow, and Tokyo as a host of the International Ballet Competition. In 1982 the US Congress passed a joint resolution designating Jackson as the official home of the USA International Ballet Competition. The competition has come to Jackson every four years since.

By the time the second USA IBC was held in 1982, the reputation of the competition had spread worldwide. The 1982 competition featured seventy-eight dancers representing nineteen countries and was featured in a ninety-minute ABC/PBS film, *To Dance for Gold,* which aired around the world. The second competition also saw its first defection, that of Chinese dancer Lin Jianwei. But the most exciting event for the home crowd in 1982 was the performance of Jackson, Mississippi's own Kathy Thibodeaux. Thibodeaux took home the senior silver medal, thrilling Mississippi audience members who cheered for "their" dancer.

"When I think back over past competitions, I remember that as a very happy moment," said USA IBC's Executive Director Sue Lobrano, who joined the IBC in 1980 and has served as its executive director since 1986. "In a way, we felt like Kathy belonged to all of us."

In the years following the competition continued to grow. The 1986 USA IBC featured eighty-nine dancers from twenty-six countries, including the first Soviet competitors to dance at the event. In 1994 131 competitors from thirty-eight countries participated, the International Dance School was filled with more than three hundred enthusiastic students from twenty-six states and five countries, and Hillary Rodham Clinton served as the event's honorary chair.

In an emotional ceremony held during the seventh competition in 2002, Thalia Mara was presented with a Lifetime Achievement Award and a gold medal for her long career in the arts, which included spearheading the effort to locate the USA IBC in Mississippi. Mara's many accomplishments also included founding the first ballet company in Mississippi that paid its dancers, the Jackson Ballet, which was later renamed Ballet Mississippi. She authored eleven books on ballet, and many of her students went on to enjoy professional careers in dance. In 1994 the Jackson Municipal Auditorium was renamed Thalia Mara Hall.

Thalia Mara died in 2003, but her legacy lives on in the USA International Ballet Competition. Over the years the IBC has grown in prestige and earned acclaim as a major cultural and performing arts event worldwide. Helsinki, Finland, eventually replaced Tokyo as one of the four primary host cities, and today, international ballet competitions are held worldwide, yet the USA IBC in Jackson, Mississippi, remains one of the oldest and most respected dance competitions in the world. Many USA IBC alumni have gone on to dance with prestigious companies, including the American Ballet Theatre, Hong Kong Ballet, Boston Ballet, and others.

In 2010 the USA IBC featured one hundred competitors from thirty-one countries and attracted more than 34,000 spectators from forty states and ten countries. The two-week event generated an economic impact of $10 million for the state of Mississippi and introduced yet another generation of Mississippians to the world of dance.

JUSTICE FOR MEDGAR EVERS

1989

Just after midnight on June 12, 1963, Medgar Evers, a thirty-seven-year-old insurance agent and field secretary for the NAACP, was shot and killed by a sniper in the driveway of his modest home in Jackson, Mississippi. Evers had just returned from a meeting at a nearby church; he was shot with his arms full of t-shirts bearing the message "Jim Crow Must Go." Evers's wife and three small children heard the shot and saw Evers collapse in the driveway. He was pronounced dead at a local hospital an hour later.

A World War II veteran and a graduate of Alcorn A&M College (now Alcorn University), Evers had been a prominent figure in Mississippi's integration movement. In 1954 he was appointed the NAACP's first field secretary in Mississippi and was responsible for organizing black boycotts of businesses that practiced discrimination, setting up new chapters of the NAACP, and investigating racially motivated crimes. In the weeks before his murder, Evers had received death threats and a Molotov cocktail had been pitched into the Evers family's carport. Days before his murder, Evers warned his wife,

Myrlie, and their three children not to sit in front of the windows in their own home.

Just hours after the murder, Myrlie Evers spoke eloquently about her husband and the cause he believed in, saying, "I am left without my husband and my children without a father, but I am left with strong determination to try to take up where he left off. And I come to make a plea that all of you . . . will, by his death, be able to draw some of his strength, some of his courage, and some of his determination to finish this fight. Nothing can bring Medgar back, but the cause can live on. . . . We cannot let his death be in vain."

A fertilizer salesman and white supremacist named Byron De La Beckwith was tried twice for the murder of Medgar Evers in 1964. The cases were vigorously prosecuted by District Attorney William Waller, a future Mississippi governor who said, "Murder is murder. It makes no difference whether a man is rich or poor, tall or short, white or black."

Despite compelling evidence that Beckwith had lain in wait for Evers and then shot him in the back with a high-powered rifle, both trials ended in hung juries and mistrials. The lack of a verdict came as a surprise; both those supporting integration and those opposed to it had predicted Beckwith would be acquitted. Segregationists proclaimed his innocence, and even those who believed him to be guilty also believed that no white man would ever be convicted of killing a black civil rights activist in Mississippi. The fact that the jury could not agree to acquit was actually viewed by some as a sign of positive change in Mississippi.

After the first mistrial in February of 1964, Myrlie Evers said, "The very fact the jurors could not agree signifies something. . . . To my knowledge, this has not happened before in Mississippi. Perhaps this should be a ray of life for both Negroes and whites. Perhaps this means we do have a conscience and are searching it." Alfred Lewis, the white national treasurer of the NAACP agreed, saying, "The verdict was frankly better than I expected from a place where men have been shot down trying to register to vote." Newspapers of the day described Beckwith as "astonished" by the mistrial, as "a quick acquittal had been freely predicted."

When a second trial three months later also ended in a hung jury and the state of Mississippi opted not to prosecute Beckwith a third time, it appeared he had gotten away with murder.

But while justice was delayed in serving Medgar Evers and his family, justice was not denied. In 1989 the Hinds County District Attorney's office reopened the Evers case when new evidence revealed that the state Sovereignty Commission, an organization formed to preserve segregation in Mississippi, had aided in Beckwith's defense by screening potential jurors. Beckwith, then seventy years old, was prosecuted for the third time in 1994. This time, more than thirty-one years after Evers's death, Beckwith was found guilty and sentenced to life in prison. Beckwith died in prison in 2001.

The opening and retrying of the Beckwith case was the subject of a 1996 feature film, *Ghosts of Mississippi*, starring Alec Baldwin as prosecutor Bobby DeLaughter and Whoopi Goldberg as Myrlie Evers. Evers's two adult sons played themselves in the movie. Describing the reenacted courtroom scene in which the guilty verdict was rendered, the late Darrell Evers said, "It was like reliving the entire thing. . . . I always wondered if I'd be able to cry in that scene. It was no problem."

Medgar Evers was buried with full military honors in Arlington National Cemetery. The hero of the civil rights movement has been honored in many ways in his home state; a street, a library, and the Jackson Medgar Wiley Evers International Airport were all named in his memory. In 2009 the Secretary of the Navy, former Mississippi Governor Ray Mabus, announced that the USNS *Medgar Evers* cargo ship would be named in the late activist's memory. Evers's widow christened the ship in 2011.

After her husband's murder, Myrlie Evers, later Myrlie Evers-Williams, continued to champion civil rights issues, eventually serving as the national chairman of the NAACP. Evers-Williams was tapped to deliver the invocation at the 2013 inauguration of President Barack Obama.

"We celebrate the spirit of our ancestors, which has allowed us to move from a nation of unborn hopes and a history of disenfranchised voters to today's expression of a more perfect union," Evers-Williams said in her inaugural remarks. "There are a great power of witnesses—unseen by the naked eye but all around us, thankful that their living was not in vain."

MISSISSIPPI ROLLS THE DICE

1990

Tourism in Mississippi reached new heights in 1990, when the state passed a law legalizing casino gaming. Today Mississippi is the nation's third largest casino gaming destination; only Las Vegas, Nevada, and Atlantic City, New Jersey, attract more annual visitors in search of Lady Luck. Mississippi is home to some thirty casino resorts, many offering luxury hotels, indulgent spas, multiple restaurants, championship golf courses, and headline entertainment, along with slot machines and table games like poker, blackjack, baccarat, and craps.

While 1990 marked the launch of "modern" gaming in Mississippi, the state has hosted gambling operations, both legal and otherwise, for centuries. The Choctaw, Chickasaw, and other Native American tribes who lived in Mississippi before white settlers arrived placed wagers on games of stickball, an ancient sport best described as a combination of lacrosse and football. Checkers, cards, and billiards were popular among the state's early European settlers, and by 1795, Natchez, Mississippi, was home to the Fleetwood

Race Track, where residents gathered to wager on horse races in a festive social atmosphere.

By the 1830s the Mississippi Gulf Coast had become a popular tourist destination. Many of the coastal resorts offered gambling activities, including cards, lawn bowling, and billiards. The river cities of Vicksburg and Natchez were also known for gambling. The rowdy landing at Natchez-Under-the-Hill was the notorious lair of riverboat gamblers and ladies-of-the-evening, a lawless, scandalous area referred to by an evangelist of the day as "the worst hell hole on earth."

The Mississippi Gulf Coast continued to be a fashionable resort area into the late 1800s and early 1900s. The enactment of prohibition in 1919 only served to make the Coast a more popular entertainment destination, as its waterfront location was ideal for smuggling in illegal liquor from the Caribbean islands. Dog Key, a small barrier island less than twenty miles off the Mississippi coast, became not only a popular drop-off point for illegal liquor, but also the site of a casino resort. Located in coastal waters outside United States' jurisdiction, Dog Key was the site of the Isle of Caprice Hotel and Resort, which opened its doors to visitors in 1926. A seventy-five-cent fare and a thirty-minute boat ride brought visitors to the Isle of Caprice, where roulette wheels, card games, rolling dice, and forbidden liquor waited. But while the Isle of Caprice was popular with visitors, Mother Nature was apparently opposed to gambling. The strong Gulf currents and the pressures of human traffic took a toll on the island's fragile ecosystem, gradually eating away at its sandy shores. By 1932 the Isle of Caprice was underwater and Dog Key itself eventually vanished into the Gulf.

Gambling continued in Mississippi's coastal and river towns and in back rooms throughout the state until the early 1950s, when a group of ministers and citizens convinced of the evils of gambling demanded that law enforcement officials enforce statutes in the Mississippi Law Code of 1942 that prohibited gambling. The ministers timed their public campaign to coincide with a US Senate investigation into organized crime in the casino industry. As a result of their efforts, gambling operations in the state began a slow but steady decline. When Hurricane Camille destroyed much of the Gulf Coast in 1969, gambling activities were swept away along with homes and businesses.

But gambling in Mississippi was resurrected in 1990, when the Mississippi Legislature passed the Mississippi Gaming Control Act, which paved the way for legal, "dockside" casino gaming in counties bordering the Gulf Coast and the Mississippi River, contingent on voters in those counties approving it. The law's local voting option weakened the opposition mounted by churches and antigambling groups. Voters in Hancock and Harrison Counties on the Gulf Coast and Tunica, Washington, Adams, and Warren Counties along the Mississippi River quickly said "yes."

Two years later, the Isle of Capri Casino opened in Biloxi, taking its name from the long since drowned but never forgotten Isle of Caprice. Splash Casino in Tunica County quickly followed. The grand openings of both properties were marked by long lines to get inside and cheers as the first jackpots were won. More casino resorts followed, many opening their doors before construction was complete; patrons played slot machines next to construction workers who were finishing the job. Mississippi law dictated that the waterfront casinos actually be *in* the water; while the casino hotels and conference facilities could be built on dry ground, the casinos themselves were constructed on massive barges just off shore. The "off shore" locations were barely detectable to patrons, who could rarely tell that the vast, 24/7 pleasure palaces were afloat. Casinos also opened on Choctaw Indian reservation land in inland Philadelphia, Mississippi, where state laws regulating casinos did not apply and profits were exempt from state taxes.

Gaming pumped new dollars and new life into Mississippi's tourism industry, attracting millions of annual visitors from outside the state and contributing millions of dollars to the Mississippi economy. Gaming also created new, well-paying jobs for thousands of Mississippians. Tunica County, once infamous as the poorest county in America, became a bustling resort community almost overnight.

The coastal gaming industry was struck a severe blow in 2005, when Hurricane Katrina devastated the Mississippi Gulf Coast. The greatest natural disaster in American history, Katrina destroyed much of the cities of Bay St. Louis, Biloxi, and Gulfport, including their casinos. Many of the massive casino barges broke free of their moorings and floated inland, crushing hotels, homes, and businesses in their paths. The casinos shut down or destroyed by Katrina represented a loss of some $500,000 *per day* in tax revenues for the state of Mississippi.

But in the months that followed, casino gaming played an integral role in the Mississippi Gulf Coast's recovery from the monster storm, not only economically, but also emotionally. When the first casinos reopened months after Katrina, displaced workers once again had jobs, and the first patrons to line up at the door were coastal residents grateful to play a few games, savor a nice meal, and spend the night in a comfortable hotel room, enjoying an escape from the cramped FEMA trailers in which most of them were now living. The Gulf Coast's flagship resort, Beau Rivage, reopened on August 29, 2006, the one-year anniversary of Katrina, with an emotional ceremony that symbolized the resilience of the people of the Mississippi Gulf Coast. "The Beau" put 3,800 people back to work following a $550 million renovation that left the property more spectacular than ever, but as Beau Rivage President George Corchis put it, "It's not all about money and it's not all about design. It's about people."

The damage resulting from Hurricane Katrina prompted the legislature to change the law requiring the casinos to be in the water, and the shift to land-based casino construction resulted in bigger and more elaborate casino developments along the coast. Led by the casinos and the tourists they attracted, the Mississippi Gulf Coast made a slow but steady recovery.

Today, Mississippi's casinos employ some 23,000 people, generate annual revenue of approximately $2.25 billion, and account for more than $280 million in annual tax revenue. A lucrative roll of the dice, indeed.

THE NATCHEZ TRACE PARKWAY, BEGINNING TO END

2005

The Natchez Trace Parkway stretches diagonally across Mississippi, cuts a corner through Alabama, and then winds to an end in Nashville, Tennessee, following an unspoiled route through lush forests, beside sparkling streams, and into the heart of America's frontier past. In May of 2005 the final sections of the parkway, which is a national highway maintained by the National Park Service, were completed, putting a period on nearly seven decades of construction.

This timeworn scenic path, some 440 miles long and more than 8,000 years old, was originally "traced out" by buffalo, then trekked by Choctaw and Chickasaw Indians, and finally trampled into a rough road by trappers, traders, and missionaries. French maps dated as early as 1733 include the Natchez Trace; British maps of the same era refer to the Trace as the "Path to the Choctaw Nation."

The Natchez Trace began in Natchez, Mississippi, and then ran north to Nashville, Tennessee. In the late 1700s and early 1800s, traders known as "Kaintucks"—the Mississippi moniker for boatmen from anywhere north of Natchez—floated merchandise down the Ohio and Mississippi Rivers on flatboats bound for markets in Natchez and New Orleans. Once the livestock, agricultural products, and coal on the boats were sold, the boats themselves were dismantled and sold as lumber. The Kaintucks then began the return trip north on foot or horseback along the old Natchez Trace.

By 1800 as many as 10,000 Kaintucks annually trekked the Natchez Trace, each laden with pockets full of money and armed with a rifle and a bottle of whiskey. The 500-mile trip took about thirty-five days on foot, twenty days for those lucky enough to travel on horseback. The terrain was rough, and a broken leg or wandering from the rough path could spell death for the lone traveler. Inclement weather often rendered entire sections of the Natchez Trace impassable. Bandits, unfriendly Native Americans, and wild animals prowled the route, just a few of the hazards that earned the Natchez Trace the ominous nickname, the "Devil's Backbone."

One of the most notorious of the Natchez Trace bandits was Samuel Mason, a Virginia native who led a band of highway robbers and river pirates. Mason was eventually murdered by two of his own men, who hoped to claim the bounty on Mason's head. When it was discovered they were bandits themselves, however, the men were instead rewarded with a trip to the gallows; according to legend, their heads were mounted on poles along the Trace to discourage other marauders.

By 1820 some twenty frontier inns or "stands" sprang up along the old Natchez Trace about a day's walk apart. The stands offered safe accommodations for Kaintucks too weary or too frightened to continue walking in the dark of night. For around twenty-five cents, exhausted travelers enjoyed the privilege of sleeping in an open room packed with baggage, saddles, and other travelers.

From 1800 to 1820 the frontier brimmed with trade and new settlements, and the Natchez Trace was the busiest highway in the old Southwest. Even before Mississippi became a state in 1817, the Natchez Trace connected the Spanish and French Territories of the lower Mississippi River to the fledgling United States. The Natchez Trace was eventually recognized as a commercial and postal route, prompting President Thomas Jefferson to obtain a $6,000 appropriation for improvements to the pathway. Jefferson's proposal was one of the first highway construction projects in American history.

But by the late 1820s, new-fangled steamboats made upriver travel by boat faster and more efficient than travel over land, and traffic along the once busy Natchez Trace dwindled. Settlements and frontier stands along the pathway were abandoned, and with the passage of time, the Natchez Trace dissolved into the brush.

In 1905 the Daughters of the American Revolution spearheaded a campaign to mark the hundreds of historic sites along the Natchez Trace, rekindling interest in the ancient path. In 1934 US Congressman Thomas Jefferson Busby of Mississippi introduced a bill authorizing an appropriation of $50,000 to fund a formal survey of the old Natchez Trace. For six years surveyors tramped the entire length of the Natchez Trace, hacking their way through the underbrush, dodging snakes and poison ivy, interviewing local residents about the route's lost sections, and marking their steps with red paint applied to trees, fence posts, and crumbling buildings along the way. Three years into the project, the historic route was designated a unit of the National Park Service.

While the survey was still underway, the National Park Service worked with the state legislatures and highway departments of Mississippi, Alabama, and Tennessee to acquire the land needed to build the modern Natchez Trace Parkway; much of the land was donated by communities and individuals who believed in the route's importance to American history. Armed with the 152-page survey, the National Park Service and the Bureau of Public Roads (the predecessor of the Federal Highway Administration) began the task of building the parkway in August 1937, paving the first section near Canton, Mississippi.

The highway engineers and landscape architects charged with creating the modern highway followed the original route as closely as possible but also allowed the natural topography of the land to dictate the layout of the new Natchez Trace Parkway. Keenly aware of the historic worth and scenic beauty of the area surrounding the project, the parkway's designers envisioned a route they characterized as "lying lightly on the land." One of the engineers described the project as "a great privilege, as it was possible to relive portions of our early history. It was a humbling experience to realize what a great heritage had been left by those who preceded us."

Early construction work on the parkway was part of a nationwide, government-funded, road-building project designed to create jobs during the Great Depression. Workers were chosen from lists of the unemployed and paid thirty cents per hour to carve a civilized road out of the untamed wilderness. Portions of the parkway were opened to traffic as they were completed. The first park rangers stationed along the Natchez Trace Parkway were charged not only with enforcing the rules of the road, but also with herding local cows that often ended up sharing the new parkway with motorists.

Work continued despite sporadic funding for the project. In the spring of 1942, construction came to a stop when engineers and construction laborers were called to duty in World War II. Federal funds once allocated for the project dwindled in favor of other programs, and at one time, President Eisenhower considered turning the Natchez Trace Parkway over to the states it crossed to build and maintain. The 1956 launch of the National Park Mission 66 Program, a ten-year program geared toward refurbishing park roads and buildings, injected new life into the project, and additional funding became available in the 1970s and 1980s thanks to the efforts of Mississippi Congressman Jamie Whitten. The final push to finish the Natchez Trace Parkway came in 1998, when Mississippi senators Thad Cochran and Trent Lott earmarked some $71 million to complete the remaining twenty-five miles.

While the rural areas of the parkway had proven the most challenging construction-wise, the sections of the Natchez Trace near the urban areas of Jackson, Natchez, and Nashville, Tennessee, were the last to be completed. The final sections of the road, including a fourteen-mile segment between I-55 and I-20 near Jackson and an eight-mile stretch near Natchez, opened to traffic in May of 2005. Nearly seven decades after the first ground was paved, the Natchez Trace Parkway was finally complete.

Today's modern Natchez Trace Parkway closely follows the original trail. The Southern penchant for sharing good tales preserved the colorful legends surrounding the Natchez Trace, and historic markers along the parkway detail the path's romantic, adventurous, and natural history. Indian mounds, ghost towns, picnic areas, nature trails, and sunken sections of the original path beckon from just off the paved road. Nearly 39,000 of the Natchez Trace Parkway's 52,000 acres are maintained in a natural condition, with forests, fields, lakes, and streams bordering the parkway. Spectacular spring blossoms and fiery fall foliage create an unforgettable seasonal display for travelers.

Small towns and cities are located just off the road, but there are no commercial establishments or streetlights along the Natchez Trace Parkway itself, creating the illusion that travelers are once again exploring a path into the untamed frontier. Modern-day travelers of the Natchez Trace Parkway might take their cue from a marker near the ghost town of Rocky Springs, which reads, "Walk down the shaded trail and leave your prints in the dust, not for others to see, but for the road to remember."

HURRICANE KATRINA
ROARS ASHORE

2005

From Waveland to Ocean Springs, a chain of spectacular casino resorts, beachfront mansions, tranquil artist's colonies, and quaint fishing villages once overlooked the tranquil Mississippi Sound.

On Monday, August 29, 2005, Hurricane Katrina slammed into this lovely section of the Mississippi Gulf Coast. The greatest natural disaster in American history, Katrina virtually erased the coastal villages of Pearlington, Waveland, Bay St. Louis, and Pass Christian and destroyed much of the cities of Biloxi and Gulfport.

The vast, Category 3 hurricane made landfall near Bay St. Louis and Waveland, Mississippi, packing sustained winds of 125 miles per hour. Katrina transformed the calm waters of the Mississippi Sound into an angry storm surge thirty feet high and eighty miles wide, the highest and most extensive storm surge in the documented history of the United States. This three-story wall of water swept as far as twelve miles inland, drowning what little it left standing in filthy, debris-choked salt water.

Katrina left a swath of death, destruction, loss, and indescribable misery in her giant wake. Grand waterfront mansions melted into the churning waters. Massive casino resorts built on floating barges broke free of their moorings and crushed everything in their paths. Luxury hotels and condominiums were reduced to mangled piles of twisted steel and broken concrete. Bridges were swept away, rendering the towns and cities they connected along the coastline virtual islands. Highway 90, a beachfront scenic route and busy thoroughfare also known as Beach Boulevard, disappeared under tons of water, sand, mud, and debris. Centuries-old buildings and beloved coastal landmarks vanished, gone in the blink of Katrina's giant eye.

The majority of coastal residents heeded warnings to evacuate, but a few hardy souls remained. Many had survived Hurricane Camille, a monstrous, Category 5 hurricane that struck the Mississippi Gulf Coast in 1969, and they found it difficult to believe that any storm could out-storm Camille. They learned differently. As Mississippi author John Grisham later noted, "[After Katrina], I suspect Camille will soon be downgraded to an April shower."

Many of those residents who remained found themselves awaiting rescue on rooftops surrounded by the white-capped storm surge, or sometimes clinging to treetops after Katrina washed their homes into the sea. Entire houses simply floated off of their slabs; one survivor reported that his sturdy, two-story house collapsed in less than fifteen seconds. Workers at the Hancock County Emergency Operations Center in Bay St. Louis, Mississippi, wrote their names on their arms with waterproof magic markers so their bodies could be identified if they were killed on the job.

Katrina left 238 people dead in Mississippi; the storm and related flooding due to levee breaks in Louisiana claimed another 1,595 lives. Katrina wreaked havoc on the entire state of Mississippi, spawning tornadoes and flash floods, causing extensive damage as far as 200 miles north of the Coast, and leaving nearly one million Mississippians without power or telephone service for weeks. The storm cost more than 279,000 people their livelihoods when their places of employment were destroyed by the storm or driven out of business in its aftermath. The total property damage caused by Katrina was estimated at between $80 and $100 billion, primarily in Mississippi and Louisiana.

The once-vibrant Mississippi Gulf Coast was reduced to a field of rubble, bare foundations, and FEMA trailers, a shattered landscape marked only by the silhouettes of centuries-old live oaks that even Katrina couldn't topple. The trees themselves were filled with debris ranging from random items of clothing to small boats to a piano. Smashed slot machines and broken appliances littered the beach, and the smell of rotting fish and garbage filled the air in the ninety-plus-degree heat.

But mere days after the storm, signs of resilience rose from the wreckage. Some signs were literal—handwritten messages scrawled on plywood or spray-painted on water-gutted buildings that proclaimed, "We are coming back!" "We love the Mississippi Gulf Coast!" "The South will rise again!" and "Katrina won the battle, but WE will win the war!"

Within weeks of the storm, there were other tangible indications that the Coast was down but not out. Mary Mahoney's Old French House, a legendary coastal restaurant housed in a building that dated to 1737, was drowned by the storm. In the days following Katrina, one of the most inspirational sights in Biloxi was a simple message spray-painted on the restaurant's exterior wall: "WE WILL OPEN." A few months later, the entire Coast celebrated when the word "will" was replaced by the word "ARE." With no tourists or paying customers to serve, Mary Mahoney's owner dished up gumbo for thousands of displaced residents and relief workers.

Biloxi's Beauvoir, the gracious retirement home of Jefferson Davis, President of the Confederacy, suffered extensive damage. More than $500,000 worth of irreplaceable artifacts was lost, but more than 3,230 items—some as small as poker chips and as delicate as glassware—were recovered from the mud and debris. According to Beauvoir's curator, "We were worried about looters, but with all the slot machines lying open up and down the beach, antiques just weren't that strong of a draw."

The Marine Life Oceanarium in Gulfport, Mississippi, was destroyed by Katrina, and eight dolphins living at the marine park were washed out to sea when the storm surge flooded their tank. One of the most moving post-Katrina moments came when the dolphins' frantic trainers took a boat into the Mississippi Sound two weeks after the storm to search for the dolphins. The trainers called and whistled, and the eight dolphins responded, swimming to the boat for a joyful reunion. Several of the park's resident sea lions were also rescued from residential swimming pools and flooded subdivisions miles inland.

For months following Katrina, relief workers and volunteers poured into the Mississippi Gulf Coast from multiple states and countries. Initial efforts focused on delivering food, water, ice, and basic supplies, then moved into massive cleanup efforts, and finally, into rebuilding. In October of 2005 a group of celebrities, including Mississippi natives Sela Ward, Morgan Freeman, Faith Hill, and B. B. King, staged a televised benefit concert called "Mississippi Rising" that raised more than $15 million in relief funds. Best-selling author Grisham and his wife established a charitable fund to help rebuild the Coast with a personal donation of $5 million.

A volunteer group from Pennsylvania staged a homecoming dance, complete with dresses for the girls and suits for the boys, for students at Long Beach High School in Long Beach, Mississippi, who had lost everything in Katrina. As one Long Beach student said, "It's not so much the homecoming, it's that people are coming to help and we don't even know them. They totally captured us by the heart with their generosity and unconditional love. You hear a lot about southern hospitality, but they brought northern hospitality down here to us."

The outpouring of support raised spirits as well as walls and helped rebuild lives as well as homes. As one Mississippi Katrina survivor said, "We have a lot of good friends who left, and they might not come back because it's so hard to rebuild. But a dear friend came back for a visit, and I told her I really felt sorry for her because she was missing all of these miracles."

The Mississippi Coast gradually rebuilt. While the area would never be the same, in many ways, residents vowed, it would be better. The reopening of the Coast's casino resorts was a major milestone in the recovery process. On August 29, 2006, the one-year anniversary of Katrina, the Gulf Coast's flagship resort, Beau Rivage, opened following a $550 million lobby-to-penthouse renovation. Homes and businesses followed suit, and today, the Mississippi Gulf Coast is once again a dynamic resort area.

The Hurricane Katrina Memorial stands watch over Biloxi's Town Green off Beach Boulevard, a stone monument honoring the Gulf Coast victims of America's greatest natural disaster. But while the memory of Katrina and all she cost the Coast will never completely fade, the people of the Mississippi Gulf Coast have largely managed to transform Katrina from disaster into triumph. Once a name that evoked images of catastrophic destruction, "Katrina" now conjures images of a courageous, resilient people and a proud, vibrant culture that refused to be defeated by a mere hurricane.

As Marsha Barbour, former first lady of Mississippi said, "I have been blessed to witness first-hand the very best in humanity. Mississippi's recovery from the worst natural disaster in American history is showing the world how great our people truly are."

THE UNIVERSITY OF MISSISSIPPI— THE FAIREST OF THEM ALL

2011

The national spotlight fell on Mississippi in 2011 when *Newsweek* magazine named the University of Mississippi, affectionately known as "Ole Miss," the most beautiful college campus in America. *Newsweek* went on to describe the Ole Miss student body as the most beautiful collection of students in the nation. The *Fiske Guide to Colleges 2013* also named Ole Miss one of the most "interesting" universities in America, citing its academic quality, social life, and yes, its campus and student body.

While alumni and fans of other colleges (including archrival Mississippi State University) might disagree, the recognition came as no surprise to Ole Miss supporters, who have touted the scenic beauty and southern charm of the Oxford, Mississippi, campus for generations, and who help perpetuate the saying that "Ole Miss redshirts Miss Americas."

Oxford, the postcard-pretty small town that is the home of the university, has also earned its share of accolades. *Travel + Leisure* named Oxford one of "America's Coolest College Towns," and *Smithsonian* magazine called Oxford one of the "Twenty Best Small Towns in America." Oxford's original city fathers would be proud. Back in 1837 they chose the name "Oxford" for their town in hopes of improving their chances of landing Mississippi's first public university. Their efforts were successful; the University of Mississippi welcomed its first students in 1848.

The university has closed its doors only once since, when the entire male faculty and student body marched away to fight in the Civil War. The wounded from the fierce battles of Shiloh and Corinth were treated in the university's graceful buildings, and legend has it that spiteful Union troops rode their horses through the university's most hallowed halls. A handful of Ole Miss's original buildings survived the 1864 torching of Oxford, including the Lyceum, a stately, white-columned, Greek Revival structure that serves as the campus focal point and the Ole Miss logo.

Perhaps the university's most famous and loveliest feature is the ten-acre, oak-studded retreat known as The Grove. Normally a peaceful spot for strolling, counting tulips, or relaxing in the shade, The Grove is packed with enthusiastic tailgaters on Southeastern Conference football game weekends. Ole Miss fans break out the china, silver, and candelabras for the pregame festivities; for really big games and rivalry matches, bartenders, waiters, and big-screen TVs are the norm. Football is serious business at Ole Miss, with a student game day dress code that includes blue blazers and ties for the gentlemen and dresses and high heels for the ladies.

In fact, it was football that first called national attention to the splendor of the Ole Miss campus. In the 1950s and 1960s, the Ole Miss Rebels were a gridiron powerhouse. The Rebels claimed national football championships in 1959, 1960, and 1962, and Southeastern Conference titles in 1954, 1955, 1960, 1962, and 1963. Sportswriters from around the country flocked to Ole Miss to cover the team and in the process also discovered the beauty of the campus and the Ole Miss coeds.

A *Sports Illustrated* article from 1960 titled "Babes, Brutes, and Ole Miss" noted, "In every region of this country people have fond, often charming and usually faintly ridiculous notions about the characteristics they possess. . . . Sometimes it does happen that reality lives up to the legend. There probably is no better proof of this than the 5,300 students who are attending the University of Mississippi. The young men at Ole Miss are astonishingly broad-shouldered and happily carefree. They are friendly and courteous, but there is a slight swagger about them, and they walk the land as if they own it. The young women at Ole Miss are softly pretty, and they smile often and cut their eyes when they say hello, and it is no wonder at all that in rapid succession two of them have been chosen Miss America. The wonder is that girls from other regions even have a chance . . ."

The article went on to describe the Ole Miss campus, saying, "The gently rolling, well-tended square mile of campus at Oxford, Mississippi, could not be anywhere except in the Deep South. There are magnolias scattered among the elms, oaks, redbud and dogwood trees, and on flat and sultry days their fragrance is everywhere, just as sentimental novelists claim. Mockingbirds sing in the trees, and on quiet nights when the moon is riding high, katydids fill the air with a soft keening, and lightning bugs blink everywhere.

"There are, naturally, no flat, geometrical, and glass-faced buildings at Mississippi. Even the newest of them are Georgian or modified Georgian, and two of the surviving four antebellum buildings are Greek Revival, with tall white columns which gleam in the moonlight or look cool and gracious when struck by the dazzling sun."

While the fortunes of the Rebel football team have waxed and waned over the five decades since that article was penned, Ole Miss's reputation for beauty and grace has never faded and has, in fact, only grown stronger and more legendary as the years have passed. In 2007 *Sports Illustrated* named Ole Miss the nation's No. 1 tailgating school based in large part on the atmosphere, charm, and tradition of The Grove, while *Sporting News* called The Grove "the Holy Grail of tailgating sites."

Even some rival schools praise the beauty of the campus and its students. When the University of Texas played Ole Miss in football in Oxford in 2012, a columnist for the Texas Burnt Orange Nation website wrote, "Let me assure you, all the Twainian tales of grandeur that you've heard regarding 'The Grove' being the greatest tailgating experience on earth are not only true, but probably grossly understated. There are no words to truly do it justice . . .

"What sets The Grove apart is the pageantry of it all, and that starts with the ladies. When they say the women are so good looking at Ole Miss that they can redshirt Miss America there, they're not wishful thinking. And it's not just that they're good looking, it's the effort and lengths they go to stick out in a cauldron of eye candy. Think social Darwinism, the All-Stars edition. Between the painted on dresses, high heels, and hair to match, just about every female mingling about is dressed like they're late for their best friend's wedding. Ensembles that would seem completely impractical and out of place at just about any other football venue in the country are basically their dress code. Their male counterparts don't go to quite those lengths, but it's definitely business casual for many and it's not uncommon to see a dapper dandy clad in a dinner jacket and a bow tie."

Lest outsiders think Ole Miss is all show and no substance, the university's administration is quick to point out that Ole Miss is also recognized for academic excellence, including an Honors College ranked among the top three in the country, twenty-five Rhodes Scholars, and a ranking by *Forbes* as one of the best-value universities in America. In the quest to find both beauty and brains, the University of Mississippi is the place.

MISSISSIPPI FACTS AND TRIVIA

- Based on income tax returns documenting charitable contributions, Mississippians are the most generous citizens in the United States.

- Viking Range Corporation, the company that introduced high-end commercial cooking appliances for the home and made stainless steel ranges, dishwashers, and refrigerators all the rage, was founded in Greenwood, Mississippi.

- Famous musicians who hail from Mississippi include Jimmy Buffet, Bo Diddley, Pete Fountain, Faith Hill, Robert Johnson, B. B. King, Elvis Presley, Charlie Pride, LeAnn Rimes, Jimmy Rodgers, Ike Turner, Conway Twitty, Muddy Waters, and Tammy Wynette. Bob Pittman, the founder of MTV, is also a Mississippi native.

- Mississippians are fond of saying, "We may not be able to read, but we sure can write." Works by Mississippi authors Margaret Walker Alexander, Nevada Barr, Larry Brown, William Faulkner, Shelby Foote, John Grisham, Carolyn Haines, Thomas Harris, Greg Iles, Willie Morris, Kathryn Stockett, Eudora Welty, and Tennessee Williams would certainly seem to back up that claim.

- Football greats Brett Favre, Archie Manning, Steve McNair, Deuce McAllister, Walter Peyton, and Jerry Rice are all from Mississippi. New York Giants quarterback Eli Manning grew up in New Orleans, but played college ball at the University of Mississippi.

- Actors and entertainers from Mississippi include Morgan Freeman, James Earl Jones, Sela Ward, and Oprah Winfrey.

- Mississippi is home to more churches per capita than any other state.

- New Orleans may have made it famous, but Mardi Gras was first celebrated in the New World in Mississippi. The original "Fat

Tuesday" was observed in 1699 by explorer Pierre Le Moyne d'Iberville and his crew at Fort Maurepas in Ocean Springs.

- The state of Mississippi has produced thirty-one Rhodes Scholars—twenty-five from the University of Mississippi, five from Millsaps College, and one from Mississippi State University.

- On December 7, 1874, the Jesse James Gang held up Corinth, Mississippi's Tishomingo Savings Bank, escaping with $15,000.

- Barq's Root Beer was invented in 1898 by Edward Barq of Biloxi.

- The national 4-H Club was founded in Holmes County in 1907.

- Mississippi was the first state in the nation with a planned system of junior colleges.

- Famed hatmaker John B. Stetson honed his skills at Dunn's Falls near Meridian. It was here the haberdasher designed his most popular creation, a men's hat known simply as "the Stetson."

- Before putting down roots on the Mississippi State University campus, a sycamore tree planted on the MSU campus flew to the moon on an Apollo mission as a sapling.

- Columbus, Mississippi's Sanderson Plumbing Products, Inc., was the exclusive supplier of toilet seats for the space shuttle.

- In 1992 Tunica County boasted twenty hotel rooms. A dozen Las Vegas–style casinos later, the county is home to more than 6,000.

- Topsoil in the Mississippi Delta is an average of 132 feet deep and in some spots reaches as deep as 350 feet.

- Jackson's Malaco Records is the world's largest gospel music recording label.

- Neatniks worldwide owe a debt of gratitude to Harry Cole Sr. of Jackson, the inventor of Pine-Sol.

- The Parent Teacher Association (PTA) was founded in Crystal Springs in 1909.

- The Waterways Experiment Station in Vicksburg is the Army Corps of Engineers' largest research, testing, and development facility.

- The world's first can of condensed milk was produced in Liberty, Mississippi, by inventor Gail Borden.

- A plane carrying the rock group Lynyrd Skynyrd crashed just south of McComb on October 20, 1977, killing six people.

- Columbia's Walter Payton was the first football player ever featured on a Wheaties cereal box.

- Hattiesburg's Camp Shelby is the largest National Guard training facility in the United States.

- Leontyne Price of Laurel was the first African American to achieve international stardom in the world of opera, performing with the New York Metropolitan Opera.

- Astronaut Fred Haise of Biloxi was aboard the ill-fated flight to the moon immortalized in director Ron Howard's *Apollo 13*. Haise was played by actor Bill Paxton.

- Confederate president Jefferson Davis was restored to US citizenship in 1978 during the presidency of Jimmy Carter.

- The rarest of North American cranes, the Mississippi sandhill crane, lives in a protected area in the grassy savannahs of Jackson County. The county's annual Crane Festival attracts naturalists from around the country.

BIBLIOGRAPHY

Hernando de Soto Crosses the Mississippi River (1540)

Bio.True Story website. www.biography.com.

Catholic Encyclopedia website. www.newadvent.org.

Personal visits by the author to the DeSoto County Museum and DeSoto County Courthouse in DeSoto County, Mississippi.

The Legend of the Singing River (1763)

Ancestry.com website. www.genealogy.com.

Busbee, Westley F., Jr. *Mississippi, A History.* Harlan Davidson, Inc., 2005.

Kirkpatrick, Marlo Carter. *Mississippi Off the Beaten Path.* Guilford, CT: Globe Pequot Press, 2010.

The Arrest and Arraignment of Aaron Burr (1807)

Busbee, Westley F., Jr. *Mississippi, A History.* Harlan Davidson, Inc., 2005.

Federal Judicial Center website. www.fjc.gov.

Historic Valley Forge website. www.ushistory.org/valleyforge/served/burr.html.

Letter from Cowles Mead, acting governor of the Mississippi Territory, to President Thomas Jefferson. Collection of the Mississippi Department of Archives and History, January 19, 1807.

PBS website. www.pbs.org/wgbh/amex/duel/sfeature/burrconspiracy.html.

Personal visit by the author and conversations with docents at Historic Jefferson College.

Stanton, Elizabeth Brandon. "The Conspiracy of Aaron Burr—a Sidelight of Mississippi History." Collection of the Mississippi Department of Archives and History, 1911.

William Johnson Is Freed (1820)

Burkett, Clark, and Jim Burnett. "The Forks of the Road Slave Market in Natchez." *Mississippi History Now,* an online publication of the Mississippi Historical Society, February 2003.

Concordian Intelligencer. Untitled clipping from the collection of the Mississippi Department of Archives and History, June 21, 1851.

David, Denoral. "Contested Presence: Free Blacks in Antebellum Mississippi, 1820–1860." *Mississippi History Now,* an online publication of the Mississippi Historical Society, August 2000.

Natchez Courier. Untitled clipping from the collection of the Mississippi Department of Archives and History, June 20, 1851.

National Humanities Center website. "Diary of William Johnson, Free Black Businessman, Natchez, Mississippi." http://nationalhumanitiescenter.org.

Personal visit by the author to the William Johnson House in the Natchez National Historical Park, Natchez, Mississippi.

Van Cleave, Timothy. "The Life of William Johnson." National Park Service website. www.nps.gov.

The Treaty of Dancing Rabbit Creek (1830)

Choctaw Nation of Oklahoma website. Treaty of Dancing Rabbit Creek (original treaty transcription). www.choctawnation.com.

Ray, Rebecca Florence. *Greenwood LeFlore, Last Chief of the Choctaws East of the Mississippi River.* Davis Printing Company, 1926.

Wells, Dean Faulkner. *Mississippi Heroes.* University Press of Mississippi, 1980.

The Gibraltar of the Confederacy (1863)

Ballard, Michael. "Vicksburg During the Civil War (1862–1863): A Campaign; A Siege." *Mississippi History Now*, an online publication of the Mississippi Historical Society. April 2004.

Civil War Women Blog. www.civilwarwomenblog.com.

Kirkpatrick, Marlo Carter. *Mississippi Off the Beaten Path.* Guilford, CT: Globe Pequot Press, 2010.

Personal visits by the author to the Vicksburg National Military Park and Old Court House Museum.

Vicksburg Campaign Driving Tour Guide. Friends of the Vicksburg Campaign and Historic Trail, Inc., 2008.

Vicksburg National Military Park – National Park Service. www.nps.gov/vick.

Where Flowers Healed a Nation (1866)

City of Columbus, Mississippi, website. cityofcolumbusms.org.

Kirkpatrick, Marlo Carter. *Mississippi Off the Beaten Path.* Guilford, CT: Globe Pequot Press, 2010.

Memorial Day website. www.usmemorialday.org.

Personal visit by the author to Friendship Cemetery.

"Yellow Jack" Invades Mississippi (1878)

Ancestry.com website. "Yellow Fever." www.rootsweb.ancestry.com.

Bellande, Ray. "Yellow Fever and Hurricanes." Ocean Springs Archives. www.oceanspringsarchives.net.

"Church of the Yellow Fever Martyrs." www.olsaintjoseph.org.

Hawkins, G. H., and Franklin Riley. "The History of Port Gibson." *The Publications of the Mississippi Historical Society.* http://claibornecountyms.org, 1909.

Moore, Sue Burns. "Claiborne County and the Yellow Fever Epidemics." http://clairbornecountyms.org.

New York Times. "Horrors of Yellow Fever: A Mississippi Town Depopulated." August 15, 1878.

Nuwer, Deanne Stephens. *Plague Among the Magnolias: The 1878 Yellow Fever Epidemic in Mississippi.* The University of Alabama Press, 2009.

PBS website. "The Great Fever." In *The American Experience.* www.pbs.org.

Biedenharn Gives the World a Coke (1894)

About.com. Inventors website. http:inventorsabout.com.

Biedenharn Coca-Cola Museum website. www.biedenharncoca-colamuseum. com.

Biedenharn, Emy-Lou. "Coca-Cola Bottled in Vicksburg." Collection of the Mississippi Department of Archives and History, 1983.

"The Coca-Cola Company: History of Bottling." www.coca-colacompany.com/ our-company/history-of-bottling.

Coca-Cola website. "Coca-Cola History: Coca-Cola Heritage Timeline." http:heritage .coca-cola.com.

Kurtz, Wilbur G. "Joseph A. Biedenharn." In *The Coca-Cola Bottler.* 1944.

Letter from Joseph Biedenharn to Harrison Jones, vice president of the Coca-Cola Company. Collection of the Mississippi Department of Archives and History, 1939.

The Birth of the Blues (1895)

Cheseborough, Steve. *Blues Traveling.* University Press of Mississippi, 2001.

"Dockery Farms and the Birth of the Blues." http://delta-blues.org.

Dockery Farms Foundation website. www.dockeryfarms.org.

Kirkpatrick, Marlo Carter. *Mississippi Off the Beaten Path.* Guilford, CT: Globe Pequot Press, 2010.

Mississippi Blues Trail marker at Dockery Farms.

Personal visits by the author to the Mississippi Delta and multiple blues sites.

Wilson, Christine. "Mississippi Blues." *Mississippi History Now*, an online publication of the Mississippi Historical Society, August 2003.

The First Teddy Bear (1902)

Buchanan, Minor Ferris. *Holt Collier: His Life, His Roosevelt Hunts, and the Origin of the Teddy Bear*. Centennial Press of Mississippi, 2002.

Jewish Virtual Library website. "Rose and Morris Michtom and the Invention of the Teddy Bear." www.jewishvirtuallibrary.org.

Kirkpatrick, Marlo Carter. *Mississippi Off the Beaten Path*. Guilford, CT: Globe Pequot Press, 2010.

Murphy, Frank. *The Legend of the Teddy Bear*. Sleeping Bear Press, 2000.

The Witch of Yazoo (1904)

Kirkpatrick, Marlo Carter. *Mississippi Off the Beaten Path*. Guilford, CT: Globe Pequot Press, 2010.

Morris, Willie. *Good Old Boy: A Delta Boyhood*. Yoknapatawpha Press, 2000.

Personal visit by the author to the grave of the Witch of Yazoo in Glenwood Cemetery.

Yazoo County Convention and Visitors Bureau.

The Great Mississippi River Flood (1927)

American Red Cross. *The Mississippi Valley Flood Disaster of 1927: Official Report of the Relief Operations*. 1929.

Barry, John M. *Rising Tide: The Great Mississippi River Flood of 1927 and How It Changed America*. Simon & Schuster Paperbacks, 1997.

National Geographic website. "Man vs. Nature: the Great Mississippi Flood of 1927." www.nationalgeographic.com.

Nowell, Princella W. "The Food of 1927 and Its Impact on Greenville, Mississippi." *Mississippi History Now*, an online publication of the Mississippi Historical Society, March 2006.

PBS website. "The Mounds Landing Levee Break." www.pbs.org.

Personal visit by the author to the Greenville Flood Museum, Greenville, Mississippi.

The Sound and the Fury (1929)

Faulkner, William. *The Sound and the Fury*. W.W. Norton & Company, 1993.

————.Speech of Acceptance upon the Award of the Nobel Prize for Literature. Transcription in the collection of the Mississippi Department of Archives and History, December 10, 1950.

Kirkpatrick, Marlo Carter. *Mississippi Off the Beaten Path*. Guilford, CT: Globe Pequot Press, 2010.

Mississippi's Writer's Page website. "William Faulkner." www.olemiss.edu.

Personal visits by the author to Rowan Oak, St. Peter's Cemetery, and the University of Mississippi.

Wells, Dean Faulkner. *Mississippi Heroes*. University Press of Mississippi, 1980.

The Natchez Pilgrimage (1931)

Arrigo, Joseph. *The Grace and Grandeur of Natchez Homes*. Voyageur Press, 1994.

Kirkpatrick, Marlo Carter. *Mississippi Off the Beaten Path*. Guilford, CT: Globe Pequot Press, 2010.

Natchez Convention and Visitors Bureau website. www.visitnatchez.org.

Natchez Pilgrimage Tours website. www.natchezpilgrimage.com.

Personal visits to Natchez by the author, including tours of the historic homes and attendance at the Natchez Spring Pilgrimage.

Writings by Roane Fleming Byrnes of the Natchez Garden Club. Collection of the Mississippi Department of Archives and History.

The King Is Born (1935)

Elvis Presley Official Website—Graceland Mansion—Memphis, Tennessee. www.elvis.com.

Kirkpatrick, Marlo Carter. *Mississippi Off the Beaten Path*. Guilford, CT: Globe Pequot Press, 2010.

Personal visits by the author to the Elvis Presley Birthplace and Tupelo Hardware in Tupelo, Mississippi, and personal visits and a high school summer spent working at Graceland in Memphis, Tennessee.

The Murder of Emmett Till (1955)

Adams, Olive Arnold. *Time Bomb: Mississippi Exposed and the Full Story of Emmett Till*. Mound Bayou, Mississippi: The Mississippi Regional Council of Negro Leadership, 1956.

Anderson, Devery. "The Emmett Till Murder." www.emmetttillmurder.com.

Atkins, Joe, and Tom Brennan. "Bryant Wants the Past to 'Stay Dead.'" *Clarion-Ledger*, August 25, 1985.

Byrd, Shelia. "Tallahatchie Apologizes for Role in Till Case." *Commercial Appeal*, October 3, 2007.

Federal Bureau of Investigation report on the Emmett Till case, February 9, 2006. www.emmetttillmurder.com.

Huie, William Bradford. "The Shocking Story of Approved Killing in Mississippi." *Look*, January 1956.

———. *Wolf Whistle*. New American Library, 1959.

Korecki, Natasha. "Family Sees Till Case Closed." *Chicago Sun-Times*, March 30, 2007.

Merriam, Eve. "Money, Mississippi." In *Montgomery, Alabama, Money, Mississippi, and Other Places*. New York: Cameron Associates-Liberty Book Club, 1956.

PBS website. "American Experience: The Murder of Emmett Till." www.pbs .org.

Transcript from *State of Mississippi v. J.W. Milam and Roy Bryant*. Circuit Court, Second District of Tallahatchie County, 17th Judicial District, State of Mississippi.

It Takes a Rocket Scientist (1961)

Clarion-Ledger. "Big Saturn Firing Pictures Future in Mississippi Area." October 20, 1961.

———. "Reluctant Residents Preparing to Leave Test Site by Jan. 10." January 6, 1963.

———. *"$25 Millions (sic) Allocated for State Space Project."* February 6, 1963.

Commercial Appeal. "Builder Explains Test Site Plans." April 11, 1963.

Daily Corinthian. "NASA's Rocket Testing Facility in Hancock County Is Largest Construction Project Ever to Hit State." February 19, 1964.

Infinity Science Center, A NASA Visitor Center website. www.visitinfinity.com.

Jackson Daily News. "Space Site Pegged at $100 Million." October 26, 1961.

"Missile Tests for Moon Probes." Clipping in the collection of the Mississippi Department of Archives and History, unattributed, undated article.

Mission Brochure. NASA's John C. Stennis Space Center, 2012.

NASA/John C. Stennis Space Center website. www.nasagov/centers/stennis.

"NASA Selects Launch Vehicle Test Site." NASA News Release, October 25, 1961.

Personal visit by the author to the John C. Stennis Space Center.

Picayune Item. "Gainesville Families Moving North." April 26, 1962.

"Rocket Test Center Site Changes Much in One Year." *Mississippi Magic,* 1964.

US News & World Report. "Space Billions—Now a Boom?" July 20, 1964.

James Meredith Integrates Ole Miss (1962)

Dewan, Shelia. "Debate Host, Too, Has a Message of Change." *The New York Times*, September 23, 2008.

Meredith, James, with William Doyle. *A Mission from God: A Memoir and a Challenge for America*. Atria Books, 2012.

Oxford: A Warning for Americans. Brochure published and distributed by the Mississippi State Junior Chamber of Commerce, October 1962.

Pettus, Emily Wagster. "James Meredith, Central Figure in Ole Miss Integration, Reflects on 50th Anniversary." Associated Press, October 1, 2012.

A report by the General Legislative Investigating Committee to the Mississippi State Legislature concerning the occupation of the campus of the University of Mississippi by the Department of Justice, 1963.

Various unattributed film clips in the Mississippi Department of Archives and History collection, 1962.

Williams, J. D. "Another Mississippi Story." Speech delivered October 31, 1962.

The World's First Lung and Heart Transplants (1963 and 1964)

Hardy, James D. *The World of Surgery, 1945-1985: Memoirs of One Participant*. University of Pennsylvania Press, 1986.

University of Mississippi Medical Center website. www.umc.edu.

The Neshoba County Murders (1964)

Austin, Curtis. "On Violence and Non-Violence: The Civil Rights Movement in Mississippi." *Mississippi History Now*, an online publication of the Mississippi Historical Society, February 2002.

Davis, Dernoral. "When Youth Protest: The Mississippi Civil Rights Movement, 1955–1970." *Mississippi History Now*, an online publication of the Mississippi Historical Society, August 2001.

Linder, Douglas. "Famous Trials." http://law2.umk.edu.

Lomax, Lewis. "Mississippi Eyewitness: The Three Civil Rights Workers—How They Were Murdered." *Ramparts Magazine*, 1964.

Personal visit by the author to Neshoba County, Mississippi.

The International Ballet Competition (1979)

Author's attendance at multiple performances of the USA International Ballet Competition.

The Capital Reporter. "Ballet's Best Come to Jackson." May 24, 1979.

Clarion-Ledger. "Films, Exhibits, Lectures to Be Held During IBC Week." May 27, 1979.

"DeMers, John. "IBC: Jackson's Dream Is a Reality Today." *Jackson Daily News*, June 18, 1979.

Draper, Norm, and Leslie Myers. "The Importance of International Ballet Has Yet to Be Judged." *Clarion-Ledger*, May 13, 1979.

Dunning, Jennifer. "Jackson Is Host to Ballet." *New York Times*, June 26, 1979.

Interview with Stephen Kirkpatrick, former dancer with Ballet Mississippi.

Interview with Sue Lobrano, executive director of the USA International Ballet Competition.

Moore, Dennis. "Officials Exploring Possibility of Another IBC in Jackson." *Clarion-Ledger*, July 11, 1979.

Review of programs and memorabilia from the 1979 USA International Ballet Competition.

USA International Ballet Competition website. www.usaibc.com.

Justice for Medgar Evers (1989)

"Beckwith Goes Home After Second Mistrial." Unattributed, undated clipping in the collection of the Mississippi Department of Archives and History.

Commercial Appeal. "Moral Victory Was Not Enough." February 8, 1964.

———. "Prosecutor Says Evers Case May Face Grand Jury Probe." November 1, 1989.

Crider, Bill. "Beckwith Tries to Make Bond." *Daily News*, February 8, 1964.

DeLaughter, Jerry. "Beckwith Jury Retires With No Decision Yet." *Clarion-Ledger*, February 7, 1964.

Freeman, Lee. "Medgar Evers's Contributions Discussed." *Clarion-Ledger*, June 4, 1983.

Hattiesburg American. "Medgar Evers's Widow Wants Case Reopened." October 3, 1989.

Kirkpatrick, Marlo Carter. *Mississippi Off the Beaten Path*. Guilford, CT: Globe Pequot Press, 2010.

Kraft, Beverly Pettigrew. "Grand Jury List to Include Look at Evers Slaying." *Clarion-Ledger*. Undated clipping in the collection of the Mississippi Department of Archives and History.

Memphis Press-Scimitar. "Mistrial in the Beckwith Case." February 7, 1964.

Mitchell, Jerry. "DA Joins Move to Reopen Evers Case." *Clarion-Ledger*, December 10, 1989.

Mitchell, Jerry, and Susie Spear. "Gov. Coleman Asked State to Spy on Evers, Memo Shows." *Clarion-Ledger*. Undated article in the collection of the Mississippi Department of Archives and History.

Moore, Edward. "Second Trial of Beckwith May Be Exactly Like First." *Commercial Appeal*. Undated article in the collection of the Mississippi Department of Archives and History.

New York Post. "Mrs. Medgar Evers Waits to Confront the Accused." January 29, 1964.

Remembering Medgar Evers for a New Generation. A commemoration developed by the Civil Rights Research and Documentation Project, Afro-American Studies Program, the University of Mississippi, 1988.

Scott, Gavin. "Beckwith Takes Stand as Case Nears Climax." *Clarion-Ledger*, April 15, 1964.

Shoemaker, W. C. "Beckwith, DA Match Wits." *Daily News*, April 15, 1964.

———. "DA Tries to Link Suspect, Weapon." *Daily News*, February 1, 1964.

———. "Prosecution Rests in Beckwith Case." *Daily News*. Undated clipping in the collection of the Mississippi Department of Archives and History.

Vanderwood, Paul. "Deadlocked Hopelessly." *Memphis Press–Scimitar*. Undated article in the collection of the Mississippi Department of Archives and History.

"Verdict Calmly Accepted in Jackson." Clipping from an unidentified newspaper in the collection of the Mississippi Department of Archives and History, February 7, 1964.

Worthy, William. "Defense Asks for Early Retrial Date." *The Washington Afro-American*, February 11, 1964.

Mississippi Rolls the Dice (1990)

Correspondence with Mississippi Development Authority/Tourism Division.

Mississippi Development Authority/Tourism Division website. http://visitmississippi.org.

Nuwer, Deanne. "Gambling in Mississippi: Its Early History." *Mississippi History Now*, an online publication of the Mississippi Historical Society, posted 2005.

Personal visits by the author to the casinos of the Mississippi Gulf Coast and Tunica.

The Natchez Trace Parkway, Beginning to End (2005)

Kirkpatrick. Marlo Carter. *Mississippi Off the Beaten Path*. Guilford, CT: Globe Pequot Press, 2010.

The Natchez Trace: Path to Parkway. Pamphlet by the United States Department of Transportation and the United States National Park Service, 2005.

The National Park Service website. www.nps.gov/natr.

Personal journeys by the author along the Natchez Trace Parkway.

Hurricane Katrina Roars Ashore (2005)

Bolger, Cori. "Mississippi Rising: Stars Power Relief Concert." *Clarion-Ledger*, October 2, 2005.

Grisham, John. "Mississippians Will Prevail." *Clarion-Ledger*, October 2, 2005.

Personal visits by the author to the Mississippi Gulf Coast before and after Hurricane Katrina.

Porter, H. C., and Karole Sessums. *Backyards & Beyond: Mississippians and Their Stories.* Backyards & Beyond, 2008.

Puente, Maria. "Storm Exacts a Cultural Toll: Museums, Historic Sites Lie in Ruins." *USA Today*, October 14, 2005.

Sloan, Stephen. "Voices of Katrina." *Mississippi History Now*, an online publication of the Mississippi Historical Society, August 2006.

William, Florence. "In Mississippi, History Is Now a Salvage Job." *New York Times*, September 8, 2005.

The University of Mississippi—the Fairest of Them All (2011)

Author's personal experiences as an alumna and fan of the University of Mississippi.

Brown, Joe David. "Babes, Brutes, and Ole Miss." *Sports Illustrated*, September 9, 1960.

Burnt Orange Nation website. "A Sincere Thank You to the Good Folks of Ole Miss." www.burntorangenation.com, September 18, 2012.

Travel + Leisure website. "America's Coolest College Towns." www.traveland lesisue.com.

University of Mississippi Department of Public Relations.

INDEX

ABOUT THE AUTHOR

Marlo Carter Kirkpatrick grew up in Memphis, Tennessee, but has called Mississippi home for more than twenty years. She lives in Madison, Mississippi, with her husband, wildlife photographer Stephen Kirkpatrick, and a house full of dogs and cats.

Marlo is also the author of *Mississippi Off the Beaten Path; 100 Years of Home: A History of Mississippi Children's Home Services;* and *Lost in the Amazon.* She and her husband collaborated on the coffee table books *Among the Animals, Images of Madison County, Mississippi Impressions, Romancing the Rain, Wilder Mississippi,* and *To Catch the Wind.* The Kirkpatricks' books have captured several awards, including the International Self-Published Book Award, the National Outdoor Book Award, a Benjamin Franklin Award, and three Southeastern Outdoor Press Association Book of the Year Awards.

Marlo's writing career has taken her to destinations throughout North, Central, and South America, as well as the Middle East and Africa, but she is always happy to return home to Mississippi.